Manifestes
5

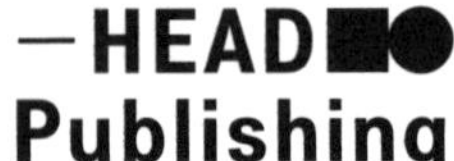

Anthony Masure
Artificial Design: Creation Versus Machine Learning

We have input the system with a data set comprising 15,000 portraits painted between the 14th and the 20th centuries. The generator then creates a new image from the data, then the discriminator attempts to distinguish the difference between an image created by a human and one created by the generator. The goal is to fool the discriminator by making it believe that the new images are real portraits. (Christie's, 2018)

This odd *mise-en-scène* of computer programmes trying to fool one another describes the conceptual process behind the work *Portrait of Edmond De Belamy* (Collectif Obvious,[1] 2018), a work generated by an 'artificial intelligence' (now referred to colloquially as AI).[2] This work was sold by Christie's for

1   Hugo Caselles-Dupré, Pierre Fautrel, Gauthier Vernier.
2   The result is an aesthetic that haphazardly plays with the classic trope of the portrait of a clerk, the codes of *non finito* of the Italian Renaissance, the brushstrokes and blurring of the avant-gardes, as well as a signature that reproduces an excerpt of the source code.

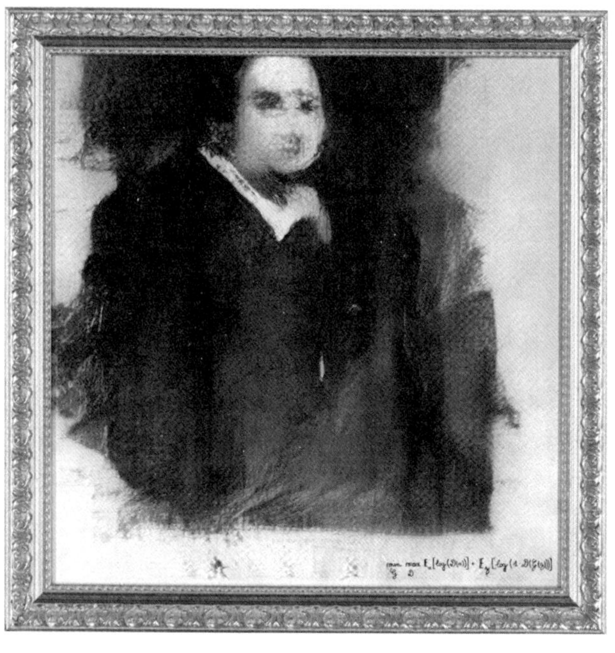

Artificial Design

a record-breaking $432,500, and drew the mainstream public's attention to machine learning technologies, opening a debate regarding the position of artists and designers in a world where machines are ostensibly able to create. This painting is in line with other initiatives such as *The Next Rembrandt* (2016), part of a communication campaign run by the advertising agency J. Walter Thompson. It took the shape of an 'original' work generated from the modelling of the styles of 346 paintings by Rembrandt (ING, 2020). A few years later, programmes such as DALL·E (2021) that produce on-demand images (illustrations, etc.) based on textual prompts, once again raised the question of the possible replacement of humans by machines, putting aside the technology's inherent economic and political dynamics.

At the dawn of the 2010s, the progress of machine learning—and more specifically deep learning—made it possible to produce computer programmes written by machines rather than human beings. Based on the analysis of enormous databases collected online (texts, images, videos, etc.), deep learning has even proven to be more efficient than 'traditional' programming when it comes to dealing with complex tasks such as form recognition and text analysis. Transposed to the fields of art and design, these issues raise complicated concerns linked to concepts of truth, authority and humanity. In order to examine these questions, it is important to begin by gaining some perspective with regards to the generic expression 'artificial intelligence' and the misconcep-

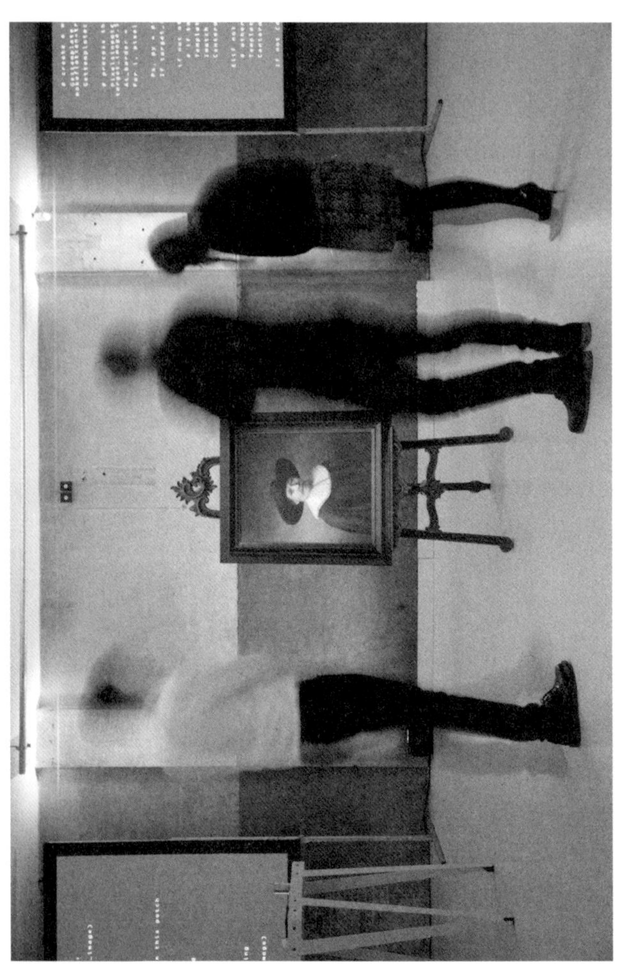

tions attached to it. The term's main pitfall is that it conceals intrinsic technical and material conditions (e.g. the concealment of primary resources and the personnel necessary to make them work), as well as software (the so-called Black Box effect) (Masure, 2019, pp.31-46). This analysis is necessary in order to highlight the fact that machine learning's dominant model (within the media landscape), deep learning, was not conceived to be intelligible but rather to be efficient. The consequence of this paradigm of profitability is the creation of a society in which productivity is the prime motivation, rather than inventiveness, ambiguity, and attention to context—all essential attributes of creative endeavours. Consequently, the media polarisation regarding the hypothetical replacement of humans by AI skirts around the crucial question that is the subject of this essay: what are the current and potential implications of machine learning for design practice?

In order to better apprehend the ways in which machine learning is part of what we propose to term 'artificial design'—to wit, an insidious subversion of the field's historic principles (notably its opposition to lower quality resulting from serial production)—this work proposes, in the first chapter (Context), to examine the psychological theories inherent to the operation of these principles. In the second portion (Political Implications), this historic overview sheds light on the tendency to reduce design to a series of schematic prototypes, in effect, a one-way model where the creative process can be automated and relegated to machines. Through the normalization of creative practices, contemporary AIs fall within the long history of creative software and the democratisation of computer access.

In order to prevent the work of designers being reduced to normative or statistical rationales, the method of research mobilised in this essay[3] consists, in the following order: in differentiating the ideas that determine the production process (in this case, AI) from their underlying concepts (automation, imitation, efficiency), in establishing the genealogy of this concept through the analysis of multiple viewpoints (designers, entrepreneurs, communicators, marketing professionals, etc.), and in synthesising the history and discourses of design projects in order to identify their underlying philosophical issues.

Contrary to the representation of design as a chain of logical processes (graphs, diagrams, timelines, and so on), this essay does not have the pretence of telling designers what to do, but rather of providing them, within the scope of their process, with critical input enabling them to analyse the current situation, or whatever they are in the process of creating. Consequently, in the third and final part of the book (Creative Potentialities), we demonstrate that machine learning technologies are shifting and redefining notions of creativity and subjectivity by automating a certain number of tasks that usually would fall within the purview of designers. For example, in the field of design, the company Zalando has been working with Google since 2016 to pre-

Artificial Design

dict fashion trends, along with using software like TheGrid.io (2014), Wix ADI (2016) and Adobe Sensei (2016) which aim to fluidify the design of interfaces, for better or worse. New ways of working with machines are emerging, as demonstrated by an associated research project led by Alexia Mathieu (Dean of Master Media Design, HEAD–Genève).[4] Mathieu interviewed a number of artists and designers; excerpts from those interviews are featured throughout this essay.

The path between political implications and creative potentialities qualifies an otherwise overly simplified division between risks on one hand and opportunities on the other. The reinforcement of power structures, for example, can cynically be seen both as a risk for marginalised groups as well as an economic opportunity. In a more fundamental sense, machine learning gives rise to a certain number of crises that require a rethinking of notions such as governance, responsibility, even the centrality of humanity and masculinity. Due to their roots in aesthetics, technique and speculation, art and design consequently have a role to play in revealing the dynamics of standardisation, and providing us with alternative relationships with machines, that transcend their instrumentalisation.

3   Here we use the formulation established by researcher Alexandre Saint-Jevin in his summary of the essay *Design and Digital Humanities* by Anthony Masure (Saint-Jevin, 2018).
4   Research project: 'Design and Machine Learning: Automation Takes Command', HEAD–Genève (HES·SO), January–December 2022, see references in bibliographical notes. The interviews are indicated in this essay under the following reference: Mathieu, 2022.

1

Alan Turing's 'Imitation Game'

The relationship between computers and thought has been a part of computing since its early beginnings. The paper 'As We May Think', published in 1945 by engineer Vannevar Bush, envisions, through fiction, machines that can increase their intellectual capacities, preventing humanity from sliding into a deadly nuclear war. Here, the delegation of intellectual operations to machines is not intended to replace humans, but enables them to 'deprogram' themselves out of tedious tasks:

> A mathematician is not a man who can readily manipulate figures; often he cannot. He is not even a man who can readily perform the transformation of equations [...]. He is primarily an individual who is skilled in the use of symbolic logic on a high plane, and especially he is a man of intuitive judgment in the choice of the manipulative processes he employs. [...] Whenever logical processes of thought are employed—that is, whenever thought for a

time runs along an accepted groove—there is
an opportunity for the machine. (Bush, 1945,
pp. 101-108)

Through his association of the notion of intelligence with selection and intuition—rather than with the processing of information—Bush portends questions that were later examined in more depth by mathematician Alan Turing. Turing's concept of a 'universal machine' lays the foundation for computer programming, that is to say a series of logical instructions executed by a machine with the intent of attaining a predetermined objective (Turing, 1936). In 1950, Turing worked with teams at the National Physical Laboratory (NPL) to introduce one of the first programmable machines, the Automatic Computing Engine, to the public. Pushing the time-honoured philosophical distinction between the mind and the body (hardware vs. software[5]) to its height, Turing began explicitly contemplating the possibility of an electronic brain. In an article published that same year, 'Computing Machinery and Intelligence', he posited the conditions necessary to consider an electronic machine as being possessed of intelligence and, if so, how one might recognise this from a human standpoint (Turing, 1950). Turing's theoretical contributions consisted in replacing the question 'Can Machines Think?' with a scenario: 'What would happen if a machine participated in an "imitation game",

5   We owe this distinction to mathematician John von Neumann. See Saulnier, 2003.

                      Artificial Design

where it took the place of a human?' In this theoretical scenario, Turing considers that the machine can be considered to show 'human' intelligence if it manages to fool a human interacting with it more than 50% of the time (Jorion, 2000). According to this now canonical model, which has been appropriated in numerous science-fiction films (*Blade Runner, Ex Machina,* etc.), the machine is perceived as a simulator, and it matters little whether anyone is able to comprehend its internal workings:

> We also wish to allow the possibility that an engineer or team of engineers may construct a machine which works, but whose manner of operation cannot be satisfactorily described by its constructors because they have applied a method which is largely experimental. (Turing, 1950)

Distancing oneself from the intelligibility of a technical system in favour of its efficiency (the so-called Black Box effect), echoes the field of cybernetics, whose principles have determined several contemporary calculation, interface, and interactivity systems, as implemented by engineers and designers.

The birth of cybernetics is generally traced back to the publication of mathematician Norbert Wiener's work *Cybernetics: Or Control and Communication in the Animal and the Machine* (Wiener, 1948). This 'science of control' (*kubernetes*) had its roots in military ballistics (the need to adjust the trajectory of a missile in real time, without human intervention), as well as in the need to optimise the flow of aerial supply lines. It quickly spread to other applications, becoming a mental paradigm related to the individual and the sum of its social relations (Klein et al., 2013). While the Black Box concept is frequently associated with cybernetics, it actually stems from behaviourism. Following Ivan Pavlov's experiments with conditioned reflexes, psychologists John Broadus Watson (Watson, 1913, pp.158-177) and Burrhus Frederic Skinner developed behaviourism, a method created to study statistical relationships between environments and behaviours without taking into account the human psyche.

 Artificial Design

Unobservable (covert) processes take place inside a 'black box' and are therefore not a focus of research, since only the observation of 'overt behaviour' (i.e. a stimulus reaction to a noise, etc.) counts. In behaviourist learning theory, the learner is like a black box since as it is impossible —and useless—to know what is going on inside. The individual is solely the product of its environment, and only its inputs and outputs are analysed.

Wiener's theory of cybernetics borrows John von Neumann's idea that a machine (a computer) can be compared to a human brain using the Black Box concept, and also introduces the concept of feedback (Rosenblueth et al., [1943] 1995, pp. 44-56). Feedback, which consists in the dynamic modification of input and output data whose aim is to control a given situation, is not a notion that exists in behaviourism. In French-speaking countries, there is a tendency to aggregate behaviourism and cognitivism (giving rise to cognitive behavioural therapy or CBT), while in the US, cognitivism was an offshoot of cybernetics and considered as more of a critical response to behaviourism. Consequently, cognitivist theories, like cybernetics, take the input/output paradigm, not in the sense that the psyche is a black box, but rather in order to study the structure of the system responsible for the differences between input and output. Defined by Wiener as 'the entire field of control and communication theory, whether in the machine or in the animal', historically, cybernetics thus cannot be reduced either to a simple evolution of mathematics, or to a behavioural rationale (Wiener, 1948).

According to philosopher Pierre Cassou-Noguès, cybernetics expand on Turing's work towards the simulation of human neurones (Cassou-Noguès, 2009, pp.141-159). After having established the bases of the computer's internal architecture (the separation between arithmetical and logic units, the control unit, RAM, mass storage, input-output mechanisms), Von Neumann began working on the concept of cellular automata, a simulation of the process of self-reproduction at the boundary between computing and biology. Von Neumann's lectures and articles were assembled in part in the posthumous work *The Computer and the Brain* (Von Neumann, [1958] 2000) which clarifies the shift from life to machines using artificial neural networks, an explicit foreshadowing—at least in terminological terms—of the neural networks of deep learning: 'Any functioning in this sense which can be defined at all logically, strictly and unambiguously in a finite number of words can also be realised by such a formal neural network' (Von Neumann, [1948] 1966, p.309).

Although one may at first understand cybernetics as a formal mathematical reduction of the human psyche, a more in-depth study shows, on the contrary, how psychiatrist Jacques Lacan also made use of the field, as he sought to reconstruct psychoanalysis by considering cybernetics as existing beyond Shannon and Weaver's 'model of communication' and behavioural methods (Saint-Jevin, 2017). In Turing's universal machine model, it is impossible to calculate a machine's shutdown. The calculation can only exist because it is possible to delineate an incalculable zone. In other words, according to Lacan, meaning can only emerge from the machine's stoppage: 'The moment when we stop the machine is what [...] gives meaning [to the world of signs]' (Lacan, [1954-1955] 1978, p. 328). The notion of the 'state of the machine' is a decisive one. Unlike Turing's universal machine, which cannot contain its own termination (shutdown), 'effective' computing had to integrate the principle of booting (starting up) in order to reset the machine to a zero-state, 'calculation-free', response (Saint-Jevin, 2017, pp. 761-773). Given that meaning emerges from the stoppage of the machine for the subject, a 'total' machine (designed with a view to continuous operation) would, therefore, not be creative, i.e. bring forth new meaning.

The psychoanalytical reading of cybernetics was soon marginalised by the rise of behavioural approaches that consistently increased their hold upon all of human activity. In 1950, the same year that Turing's article on intelligent machines was published, Wiener expressed his concerns regarding the risks of a technological progress that could lead to 'an inhuman use of human beings' (Wiener, 1954), which continues today through the proliferation of objects and technical systems whose final aim is continuous operation, leaving the individual outside of meaning.

     Artificial Design

The Two Paths of AI:
Symbolic and Connectionist Approaches

The simulation of human neurones paved the way for an initial, 'Connectionist', approach to artificial intelligence (see the work of Warren McCulloch, Frank Rosenblatt, et al.), based on Lacanian psychoanalysis. Engineers use 'representations' of neurones that are connected by artificial synapses (following neurologist Sigmund Freud's trailblazing work on the notion of 'connected' neurones) (Saint-Jevin, 2019, pp. 99-177). This approach was met with opposition from the proponents of Symbolic logic (Marvin Minsky, Seymour Papert, Allen Newell, Herbert A. Simon, et al.[6]), who proposed a modelling of the 'universal laws' of thought through the manipulation of symbols (Cardon et al., 2018). The expression 'artificial intelligence' was coined in 1955 by mathematician John McCarthy. McCarthy and his colleagues, Marvin

6 In reality, the ideas put forth by these personalities cannot easily be assigned to such binary categories, the distinctions are much more blurred.

Minsky, Nathaniel Rochester and Claude Shannon were proponents of the Symbolic approach, which is based upon the premise that 'every aspect of learning or any other feature of intelligence can in principle be so precisely described that a machine can be made to simulate it.' (McCarthy et al., [1955] 2006). When Minsky, a cognitive scientist and researcher, criticised the calculating capacities of 'perceptrons' (the ancestors of neural networks), investors lost confidence and plunged AI into a 'first winter' that lasted from 1974 to 1980 (Minsky & Papert, 1969).

In 1982, physicist John Hopfield demonstrated that neural networks were able to learn, and he used this information in an entirely new way. While still marginalised, this approach resurfaced during AI's 'second winter' (1987–1993), which coincided with the collapse of AI's symbolic promise of 'expert systems' (decision-making tools that were supposed to imitate cognitive capacities). In the late 1980s, the research assembled by computer specialist Yann Le Cun reopened the avenue of neural networks, which proved more efficient than the Symbolic approach. For example, when applied to the automatic recognition of handwritten postal codes provided by the US Postal Service, neural logic succeeded in managing the entire operation, from the normalisation of typographic characters to their final classification (Le Cun et al., 1989, pp.541-551). As researchers Dominique Cardon, Jean-Philippe Cointet and Antoine Mazières have noted, it was the data explosion in the 2010s, characteristic of the popularisation of digital uses

 Artificial Design

and big data, that legitimated the neural approach for good. This approach has been shown to be highly effective in the treatment of a wide range of data, from voice and word to signal processing, but above all it enabled them to deal with new challenges such as spam detection, collaborative filtering used by recommender systems, stock prediction, information research and the analysis of social networks (Cardon et al., 2018).

At that point, technologies with a Connectionist approach prevailed, to the point of being conflated by the mainstream public with the far broader notion of artificial intelligence, thus creating a rather strange loop in the social history of technical sciences where the 'researchers, based upon the arrival of massive amounts of data and the development of calculating capacity, set out to reformulate the project of Symbolic artificial intelligence by reviving the idea of the adaptive and inductive machines from the cybernetics era' (Cardon et al., 2018). Nevertheless, as we shall see, the return to a Connectionist approach brought about by the neural networks of the 1980s was not based on the psychoanalytical character of historic cybernetics, but rather on older behaviourist theories , since the methodological horizon of machine learning was to increase result efficiency rather than examine how the psyche worked.

The term 'deep learning' was coined in 2006 by engineer Geoff Hinton (Hinton et al., 2006, pp. 1527-1554). Derived from machine learning, deep learning refers to a method where the machine's objective is to learn by itself—unlike 'traditional' programming using symbolic logic, where the objective is limited to executing tasks according to parameters that are predetermined by humans. Deep learning is based on a network of 'layers' of artificial neurones, inspired by the human brain, that can handle complex data via processes of feedback propagation (Kurenkov, 2015). The baseline data is essential: the more the system accumulates, the better it should perform. In order to be computed, the data must first be 'bit-sliced' in order to be converted into vectors. Thus, the layers of neurones make it possible to break down a complex task into vectorial subcategories (which are non-significant for humans). The ideal is to automate the entire process in order to reach unsupervised learning. For example, the system learns

          Artificial Design

to recognise letters before words in a text, or to determine whether there is a face on a photograph before attempting to discover the person's identity. At every stage, the 'bad' information is eliminated and sent to front-end levels in order to align the mathematical model. By comparing the raw input with tagged datasets (output), the neural network automatically adjusts its processes, rewriting itself and creating an increasingly effective computer programme. With deep learning, it is no longer human operators who set the parameters for data processing, using carefully calibrated small data-sets, but rather machines, that are entrusted with 'the task of producing pertinent predictions as they learn from data' (Cardon et al., 2018):

> The architecture of these machines is charac-terised by the fact that their interaction with the environment (the world) is so intimate that it is not necessary to endow their calcula-tors with their own agency. The proposition of cybernetics is to turn them into simple asso-ciationist black boxes that can learn and whose horizons are set by the measurement of the gap (the error) between the world and the behaviour of the machine (Cardon et al., 2018).

This quote shows, in light of what we have seen earlier, that deep learning has created a confusion between behaviourism and cognitivism, since, historically, cybernetics appears to challenge the notion of the Black Box effect. Admittedly, the latter makes use of the methods of behaviourism, but its objective is to formulate hypotheses on the ways in which behaviours are carried out. This demonstrates that, while deep learning is a product of cognitivism, it is closer in nature to behaviourism, even as it runs counter to the historical principles of cybernetics (the retropropagation of neural layers is not equivalent to the retroaction of feedback).

2

The historical study of artificial intelligence, from its roots in cybernetics to its behaviourist reformulation as deep learning, reveals that the latter mostly involves a utilitarian vision of the social body. Although it is a powerful tool for dealing with large datasets, deep learning raises many major problems:

- Generally speaking, far from being a neutral technology operating apart from power structures (states, companies, etc.), deep learning extends and reinforces these structures. Examples of 'immoral' applications of artificial intelligence are hardly lacking, such as the profiling of tastes and the generation of personalised content (Netflix, 2017), the user path analysis used for e-commerce (*New York Times, Dynamic Meter,* 2022), or the detection of drunk passengers (Uber, 2018). All are signs of technological solutionism, the concept of seeing technology as the solution to any socio-political problem (Morozov, 2013).

Contemporary AI is based upon the same ideological bases as prevailing computer science, namely a rationalisation of the perceptible (Klein et al., 2013) and the modelling of realities. In her *Atlas of AI*, researcher Kate Crawford notes: 'This epistemological flattening of complexity into a clean signal for the purposes of prediction is now a central logic of machine learning' (Crawford, 2021, p.213). Likewise, Cardon, who is a sociologist, ironically comments:

'[...] Algorithms that are supposedly predictive have not actually managed to plunge into the subjectivity of humans in order to evaluate their desires or aspirations. They are predictive because they constantly work upon the hypothesis that our future will be a reproduction of our past.' (Cardon, 2015, p.70).

- Because they are mainly made up of content collected online, the datasets of deep learning carry and reinforce social bias, particularly in terms of gender representations , and representations of Black, indigenous and people of colour (BIPOC). There is no shortage of examples: a police force seeking to predict behaviour perceived as potentially criminal (*Predictive Policing*, 2011), an American court using statistics to quantify recidivism risks, with harsher rulings against BIPOC (Department of Justice, National Institute of Corrections, 2016), a recruiting robot that discriminates against women (Amazon, 2018), or the facial recognition systems that seek to determine the gender of people online (Face++, 2018), or at airport check-ins (Detroit, USA, 2018). These embedded mechanisms of discrimination are all the more insidiously powerful because they are invisible, and they can have serious consequences for populations that are already being marginalised. According to Crawford and artist Trevor Paglen:

'[Vast datasets such as ImageNet] aren't simply raw materials to feed algorithms, but are political interventions. [...] The whole endeavour of collecting images, categorizing them, and labelling them is itself a form of politics, filled with questions about who gets to decide what images mean and what kinds of social and political work those representations perform.' (Crawford & Paglen, 2019; Keller, Gunti & Amoser, 2021, p. 83).

The ethical requirements expressed regarding machine learning, even supposing they can be modelled, are difficult to align with the variety of regulations and values of nation-states. How is it even possible to compare Chinese, American, Arab or European AIs? Should we work to 'decolonise' their patterns? (Lovink, 2022).

- Most of the researchers working on machine learning work for GAFAM (Google, Amazon,

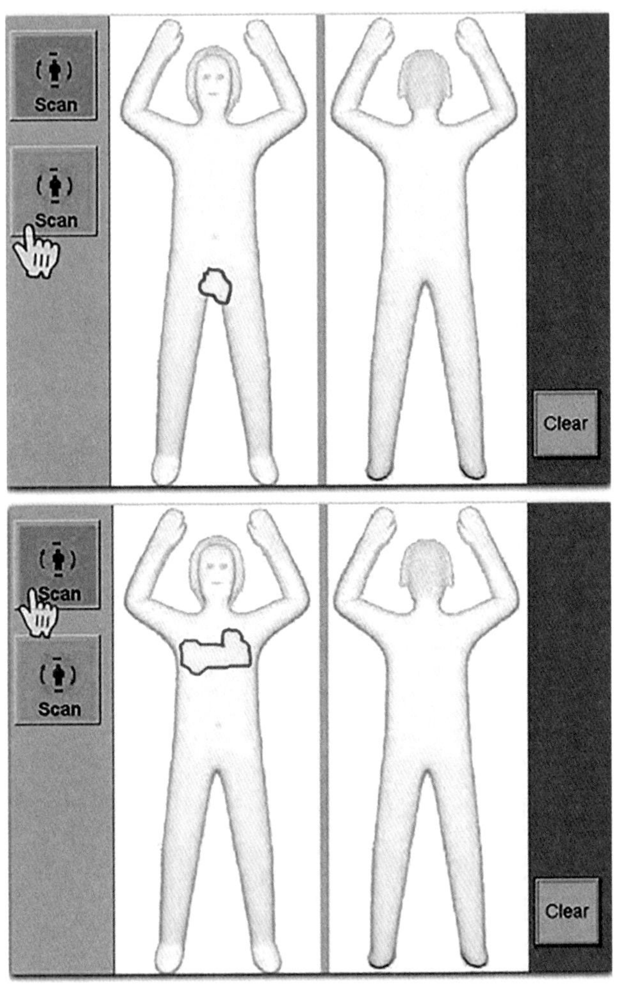

 Artificial Design

Facebook, Apple, Microsoft) or their Asian equivalents (BATX: Baidu, Alibaba, Tencent and Xiaomi). They are the only actors that can remunerate them, collect the necessary data and compute it, which only serves to reinforce their hegemony. Le Cun has been working under the aegis of Facebook since 2013 (the same year in which Hinton, his post-doctorate thesis advisor, joined Google), and is generally regarded as the inventor of deep learning. Le Cun has been developing image and conversation scanning processors that reinforce the toxic technical architectures of Facebook's advertising platform, which counts two billion users (Ertzscheid, 2018). The members of the working group AI Anarchies have pointed out that one can legitimately entertain doubts about the capacity of these large conglomerates to work for the common good:

'The ethics of AI amount to a lukewarm promise on the part of these giant groups to self-regulate Big Tech even as they forge ahead with their course towards a future of their own conception. At the same time, machine learning systems are being developed on a massive scale.' (Herrmann & Vukajlović, 2022)

• Due to the opaque nature of deep learning technologies, no one, including the programmers themselves, knows exactly how the programmes actually work. Designer Boyd Rotgans has called for increased technical transparency:

'The challenge that we must confront is the need to be transparent in the methods of decision-making, or at least to be able to say which data has been entered and which results have been obtained. If you purchase a product at the supermarket, you can read what it contains on the label and how it has been produced. It is frightening when the gulf between humans and technologies becomes too wide.' (Mathieu, 2022)

This paradigm of opacity generates a problem in terms of responsibility, since it becomes impossible to attribute blame to anyone or anything. Who or what is to blame when a programme formulates a faulty diagnosis and 'kills' a hospitalised person, or when an 'autonomous vehicle hits a person? While some people think that it is possible to create 'explainable' deep learning, this transparency would require the production of technical overlays, which are themselves questionable. On a more general level, sociologist Benjamin Bratton perceives the increasing number and layering of programme stacks as signs of the emergence of a numerical Leviathan capable of supplanting all other forms of governance and sovereignty:

'[A] certain humanism [...] still presumes its traditional place in the centre of the frame. We must let go of the demand that any Artificial Intelligence arriving at sentience or sapience

 Artificial Design

must care deeply about humanity—us specifically—as the subject and object of its knowing and its desire.' (Bratton, 2014)

It is a matter of knowing whether, under the pretext of efficiency, design ought to affiliate itself with a technical approach that works against us by making the unintelligible a prerequisite for optimisation.

- Most of the time, deep learning and machine learning are presented in a dematerialised light, flouting the burdensome ecosystem, both technical (data centres, mining of rare metals, etc.) and human, which is intrinsic to its operation. Beyond robots, deep learning cannot function without the people whom sociologist Antonio Casilli refers to as 'clickworkers', to wit, proletariat from the Global South tasked with sorting through the collected data (Casilli, 2019).

- Given their efficiency, neural networks present themselves as the only possible forms of AI, and yet the conflation of intelligence with statistical sciences, as well as the pseudo-autonomy of these technologies, should both be questioned (Moulier-Boutang & Kyrou, 2018, pp.7-15). In fact, it is significant that AI only aims to simulate a restrained sort of comprehension of human intelligence that can do nothing but function (in the fields of nudge theory, neuromarketing, and so on, for instance).

Contemporary AI relates to the ideal of the 'continuous' operation of the human psyche, undercutting other approaches, such as psychoanalysis, which, in contrast, are based on the notion of dysfunctionality.

The risk of the subjugation of human beings—their assignment to pure utilitarianism—brings us to the heart of the intersecting issues of design and simulated intelligence. As researcher Emanuele Arielli notes: 'The encounter between AI and aesthetics is crucial because aesthetics is considered a quintessentially human domain' (Arielli, 2021, ch. 1). The application of deep learning to creative occupations is but one chapter in the long history of their computerisation, and it is a convergence that is anything but easy. In an article that reviews methods of computer-assisted drawing since the 1960s, architectural historian Jordan Kauffman asserts that the transposition of formal logic to the field of design raises a number of technical challenges, but also, and above all, epistemological ones:

> Retrospectively, the transition to computing seems to have been the most complicated with regards to design itself. This is because

the creative process cannot easily be broken down into systematic, scientific, or mathematical rules that can generate exact answers, and because, for designers and architects, the expression of an idea through drawing is the primary method of creation and communication at a time during which it was necessary to attempt to conciliate computers and the practice of drawing [...]. How in the early stages of computer-assisted design, did the machine affect and assimilate the act of drawing, the process of drawing and design, as well as the drawings themselves[?]. (Kauffman, 2016)

Even as the advent of personal computers was marked by diverse and open propositions with debates on the role and place of programmes in the creative fields, dominant computer science chose a one-way street where automation and productivity took precedence: GUIs (graphic user interfaces), the annexation of design by UX Design in the 1970s, DTP (desktop publishing) and CAD (computer-assisted design) in the 1980s, the hegemony of social media (2000s), templates, guidelines, app stores (late 2000s), the digitisation of image databases and portfolios (Deviant Art, 2000; Flickr, 2004; Behance, 2005), web software prototyping (2010s), and the integration of machine learning in software (Adobe Sensei, 2016; Runway ML, 2019). These major developments outline a trajectory within which design became automated and lost its

Artificial Design

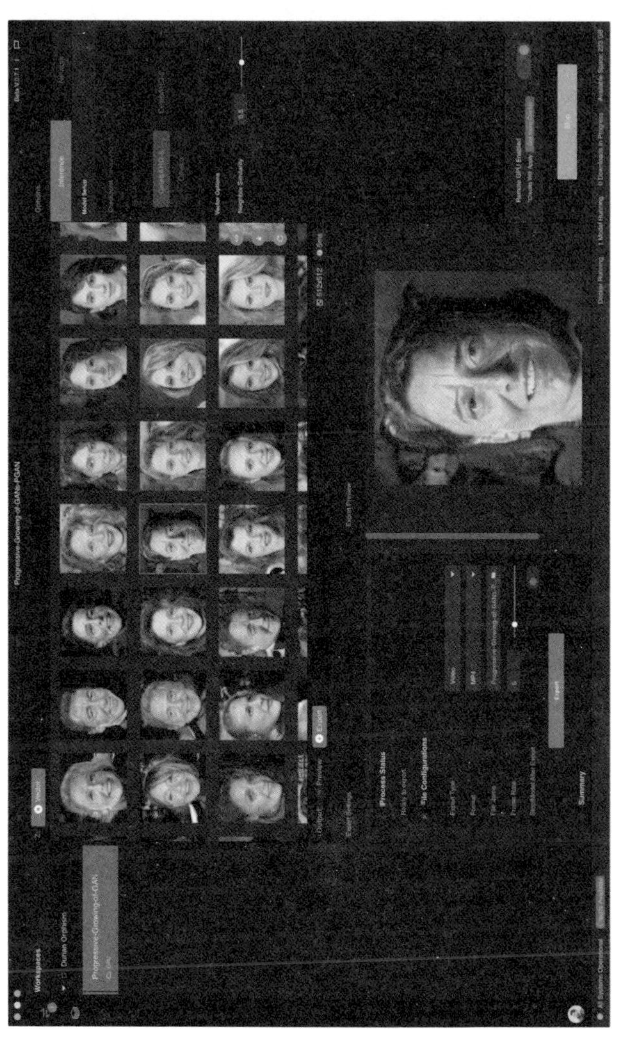

historical meaning, as inventiveness, the capacity to question context, connection with materials, and, in a more general sense, the progression through forms and uses (Masure, 2023a) were all pushed to the background. By adhering to principles of profitability, efficiency and fluidity without putting them into perspective, design, to a large extent, has wandered from the historical context of its appearance, marked by a deviation from Industrial Revolution ersatz (Masure, 2023b). The problem that arises, then, in contemporary terms, is the institution of a conflation between computer-assisted designers and designer-assisted computers. Once processes became automated, there was a risk that the machine might perform better, as artist and designer John Maeda darkly foresaw:

> It is difficult to distinguish today's computer-aided designer from the designer-aided computer. [...] Designers no longer define culture; designers must abide by a culture defined by technologists. The renowned architecture educator William Mitchell states in *Digital Design Media* (Van Nostrand Reinhold, 1991) the logical conclusion to this predicament: 'We are very close to the point [at] which the average designer may have nothing to sell that is worth anyone's money to buy'. (Maeda, 1995)

With the massive explosion of data available online and real-time tracking, data science modelling has been integrated into all fields of design (graphic design, fashion design, product design, architecture, etc.): culture in the broadest sense has become fuelled by the automated production of cultural artefacts. The deep learning technologies of the 2010s reinforced this context where the machine is no longer seen as a collaborator (a device) or an assistant (a tool), but rather as an efficient means (a plan) to replace the human factor in order to increase profitability.

With deep learning AIs, the authority of the author and his or her visual signature are challenged by programmes that are now capable of analysing and automatically synthesising (imitating) immense datasets. As has been mentioned at the beginning of this essay, systems dubbed as 'intelligent', such as OpenAI (2015), GPT-3 (2020), DALL·E (2021), Disco Diffusion (2021) or Midjourney (2022), have pushed the usability of photo effect filters and specialised DTP menus to a new level. A simple text command (prompt) is all that is required to generate a set of images by remixing previously collected vector data. The structure of prompts, which is the subject of numerous debates, varies according to the systems and their evolution. Generally, it associates themes, styles and expressions in phase with the filters and document renderers, for example: 'cosy cyberpunk futuristic room in a city during daytime with a window overlooking the skyline, ultra photoreal, photographic, concept art, 4K, octane render, cinematic lighting, highly detailed'. As graphic designer Étienne Mineur explains:

 Artificial Design

In order to master these systems, one must assi-milate the structure of these languages and know how to put the words in the 'right order' (that is to say, aligning one's language based on that of the machine), sometimes by regulating them with punctuation signs. (Mathieu, 2022)

Generally speaking, through deep learning, the machine becomes capable of associating a lexicon with forms, whether they are bitmap (based on pixels), vectorial, or three-dimensional (Apple GAUDI, 2022). This promise of creation (almost) without any explicit human intervention revives the old debate about whether a machine can be a viable substitute for a designer. According to us, this binary formulation, is an obstacle to the comprehension of the wide range of implications of machine learning. In an unequivocally-titled paper, 'If You're Worried About DALL·E Replacing Illustrators, You Don't Understand The Power of Illustration', illustrator Julien Posture demons-trates that contemporary AIs are not replacing illustrators, but rather preconceived notions of illus-tration, namely the uninspired execution of a tex-tual brief, through a recourse to one fashionable style or another (Posture, 2022). Such efforts were already on offer from microwork platforms such as Fiverr (2010) or Upwork (2015), where people from the other side of the world can provide you with a logo for five dollars. In the end, this type of approach is limited to accelerating responses to clearly formulated commands (briefs). This, how-ever, is not always obvious to many clients, notably

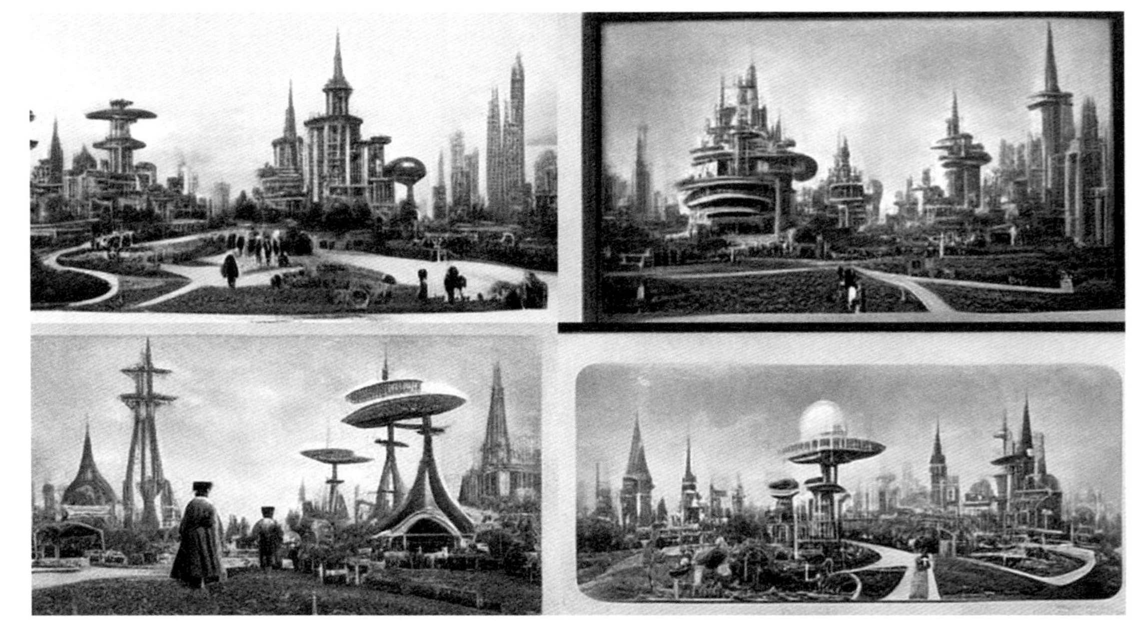

those who require an extensive exchange in order to make their needs fully understood, an amount of time superior to that allotted within the strict parameters of a brief: 'generating is not necessarily crafting' (Ertzscheid, 2022). It remains to be seen just how many clients will be conscious of this difficulty and will accordingly opt to forgo the ease of selecting options from a catalogue. One means of understanding these formatting dynamics resides in the study of the constitution of databases, which are not all open, and which strongly affect the results. Many of these systems contain lists of prohibited keywords in order to protect developers from any misadventure—an insidious form of censorship that can nevertheless be avoided through the use of synonyms. It should also be noted that the names of designers such as Philippe Starck do not appear in DALL·E, which poses major legal challenges as regards the respect of copyrights and the marketing of productions (Benhamou, 2022). Some prompt systems forbid the resale of generated images, while others, such as Stable Diffusion, place images under a free Creative Commons license (CC 0).

More fundamentally, these prompt-based programmes call to mind the Conceptual Art movement of the 1960s, where a work of art consisted of verbal intent rather than materiality, and even evoke the Book of Genesis in the Bible, where the word determines creation. However, according to designer and

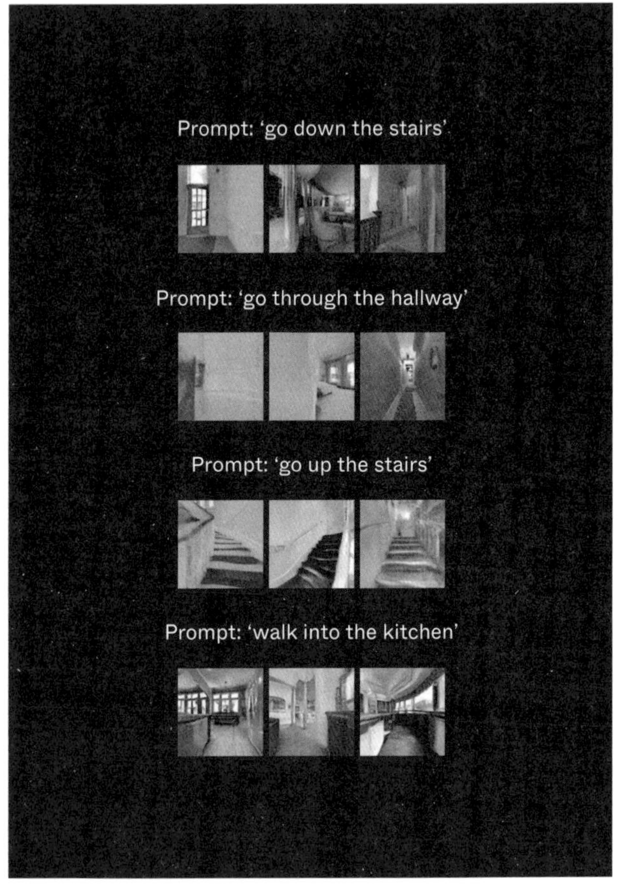
Prompt: 'go down the stairs'
Prompt: 'go through the hallway'
Prompt: 'go up the stairs'
Prompt: 'walk into the kitchen'

researcher Martin Tricaud, the verbalisation of a creative intention is by no means an easy matter:

> Using words for what we do is far more complicated than the designers of systems such as DALL·E can imagine. What's more, as sociologist Eva Illouz has shown, the verbalisation of one's intentions can bring about decisional paralysis and emotional apathy. For example, in dating apps, people are asked to use increasingly precise words to define the sort of person they are looking for, which kills some of the magic. The reason why I paint abstract works is precisely because I am unable to reason out certain things verbally. In art and design, there are non-verbal rules regarding composition and construction, and one is not constantly anticipating the intent or materialisation of a language. (Mathieu, 2022)

In the logic of prompts, the time (labour) necessary for conception no longer counts, since the latter is now relegated to machines. Rather, the emphasis is placed on finding the perfect formula to obtain the desired result, as demonstrated by start-ups charging clients for creating the text allowing the generation of a series of images by DALL·E 2 (Wiggers, 2022) or the development of dedicated programmes (Shane McGeehan, Prompter, 2022), raising the spectre of slipping into 'absolute semiotic capitalism' (Ertzscheid, 2022). On an economic level, deep learning could modify the design value chain by reducing production costs (a lowering of

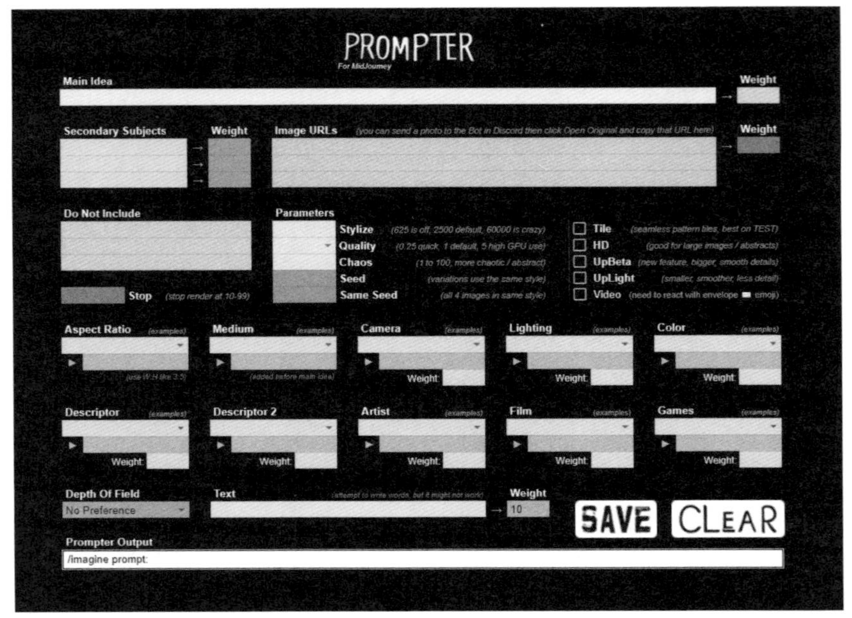

Artificial Design

perceived value), and increasing that of consulting (difficult to model and consequently, to automate). One might even arrive at a situation where there is a partition of sorts, with, on one side, 'elite' design, operating through commissions with high added value where a healthy dose of freedom and originality is expected (as is the case in the cultural sector), and, on the other, 'average' design, where AIs take charge of cookie-cutter commissions, to the detriment of designers working in that segment of the market. To avoid this risk, designer Boyd Rotgans notes that 'doing something new with machine learning, not simply repeating the same old thing, requires a great deal of technical expertise, which presents a major challenge for graphic designers' (Mathieu, 2022).

[Fig. 7] Shane McGeehan, software interface

In the case of prompts, it is not design in the strongest sense of the term (questioning a context, reformulating a request) that deep learning technologies automate, but rather its reduction to the generation of visual artefacts that resemble what already exists. Furthermore, this is a schematic and biased view of the past, since the data that serves as a baseline for the results is limited to content that is well-represented online (Crawford & Paglen, 2019). This of course excludes many periods and cultural contexts. It is striking to observe that this tendency to automate the production of cultural products (works of art, and so on) under the guise of innovation, in fact goes hand in hand with the return of the old concept of imitation. The two artistic examples mentioned in the introduction (*The Next Rembrandt,* 2016; *Portrait of Edmond De Belamy,* 2018), which use cutting-edge technology and are acclaimed by the media as innovative, could, due to their desire to imitate the canonical works of art history paradoxically be placed in the tradition of mid-19th century Academic art. One could even go further back and evoke the traditions of monastic scribes, for whom the copying of books was akin to a teaching aid from which an artistic language could emerge.

These brief historical references show that, contrary to what one might believe in the wake of the fantasies of agency and separation that surround them, deep learning technologies are less concerned with singular craftsmanship than by the efficient reproduction of the past. This tendency echoes researcher Jacques Perriault's *effet diligence* (or stagecoach effect), according to which 'older protocols are frequently applied to new technologies' (Perriault, 2000). The case of the invention of photography can also help to shed light on our contemporary situation. When it appeared at the end of the 19th century, photography initially imitated the codes of painting, aiming to become a faster way of producing images. Photography as art only emerged once it began to diverge from pictorial codes (Huyghe, 1999). Therefore, according to us, the question of the acceptance of a world fashioned by AI is less one of the replacement of humans by machines than one of camouflage: an environment in which one cannot distinguish whether something has been produced or not by simulated intelligences. It is only possible to automate what has been simplified beforehand, which brings us back to Turing's intuitive reflection: 'as soon as any technique becomes at all stereotyped it becomes possible to devise a system of instruction tables which will enable the electronic computer to do it for itself' (Turing, 1947).

According to philosopher Pierre-Damien Huyghe, behind this desire to mechanise all actions in the name of profit, and the resulting fascinating and even magical-seeming display, lies the flip side—the homogeneous results:

> In the world of mechanisation, whether it is a matter of working or merely consuming, the resulting uniformity of time is a concern. It is a world governed by constant cadences, the identical, and the repetitive. While the modes of production might be original, the production itself is uniform. Thus, one might wonder whether the abundance of industrialised society, when regarded in depth, and despite all its attempts to deny this, is not haunted by the risk of monotony. (Huyghe, 2013)

In order to fray a path less travelled that is more sustainable than this tendency towards the homogenisation of innovation, we must transcend the opposition of human vs. machine, that is, the idea of a 'replacement' of designers by supposedly intelligent programmes. When posed in a binary manner, this question, as Crawford demonstrates, just leads us into an impasse:

> Over and over, we see the ideology of Cartesian dualism in AI: the fantasy that AI systems are disembodied brains that absorb and produce knowledge independently from their creators, infrastructures, and the world at large. These illusions distract from the far more relevant

     Artificial Design

questions: Whom do these systems serve? What are the political economies of their construction? And what are the wider planetary consequences? (Crawford, 2021, p.215)

Behind the magical aspect of the overall idea of an 'artificial intelligence' (i.e. the fantasy of the mechanisation of a normative psyche), the workings of deep learning reduce learning to training, that is, to the internalisation of behaviours and the imitation of models. The logic of mechanisation, as applied to computing, boils down to the freezing of language, since its formalisation is a prerequisite in order to be able to submit it to calculation (this is why it is called a 'formal language'). As philosopher Jean Lassègue notes, language is never definitively set once and for all, rather, it should be seen as a substance that is unceasingly reworked from the inside through practices and literature:

> The manner in which language renders metaphors from its material is such that an encyclopaedic approach to the lexicon will never suffice to render language completely intelligible because the transformation of its mode of production is its very engine of change. When you use words, you are simultaneously acting upon the words you select and you transform the meaning of the word in question. (Lassègue, 2018).

With deep learning prompts, the work performed by language is circumvented by the effortless passage from word to image: that is, to the extent that knowing how to speak the language of the machine already requires an effort. The replacement of aesthetics (the science of perceptions) by a verbal register entails the risk of remaining in literality (in the total act of showing) rather than in the transformation of meaning (in interpretation and even subversion). One example would be that an illustration is not merely the servile creation of an image from a text, but rather a visual game that makes use of ellipses and unsaid things, blanks that the reader must fill in themselves.

 Artificial Design

The Conflation of
Creation and Production

The use and media coverage of DALL·E are both based on the seductive power of what feels like magic, to wit, a result whose mechanics are difficult to explain and whose various elements are organised in such a way as to divert and avoid any questions. Although the execution time of prompt systems is faster than human labour, it is not instantaneous. Just as a camera 'works' alone for a fraction of time, the necessary time required for the generation of images paradoxically opens up an interval for daydreaming, a few minutes during which one wonders just what the machine will do. However, this lapse of time can be reduced by paying the systems that enable this—the aim being immediacy.

In order to better understand the foundations of the fantasy of engendering an idea free of material vicissitudes (the pitfalls of execution), it is instructive to look back to the appearance of recording devices in the 19th century. Poet Charles Baudelaire saw photography, then a nascent art, as a challenge to established arts such as painting. He virulently denounced the pretensions of the mechanical to creating art:

> These are deplorable days, when a new industry has appeared, one which will make no small contribution to [...] ruining what remains of the divine in the French spirit. The idolatrous crowds have thought up an ideal worthy of them [...]: [...]'We think that art is and cannot be anything but the exact reproduction of Nature [...]. Consequently, the industry that provides us with a result that is identical to Nature would be the absolute in art. [...] Since photography gives us all the guarantees of exactitude we desire (that is what these insane people believe), hence art is photography.' From that moment on, this lowest common denominator of society raced, like a single Narcissus, [to reproduce] and contemplate their trivial images on metal. These new adorers of the sun are seized by a folly, an extraordinary fanaticism. (Baudelaire, [1859] 1999)

In a comment of this text, philosopher Pierre-Damien Huyghe hypothesised that Baudelaire rejected photography as art because it introduced 'an intense desire for exactitude' among the masses (Huyghe, 2022, pp.71-72). On the contrary, Walter Benjamin saw in it the possibility of the foundation of a new culture where the process of reproduction would not be concealed but rather recognised (since exact reproduction does not exist).

 Artificial Design

These old concepts of mechanics and exactitude are not totally behind us, since they still feed the fantasies surrounding AI, which promise the accurate and effortless reproduction, not of Nature, but of the past. In order to gain a better understanding of these issues, it is important to distinguish the notions of 'creation' (i.e. the romantic vision of an *ex nihilo* inception) and 'production' (the attention given to technical methods and social relationships). Firstly, it should be noted that the concept of creation is historically recent in the field of art:

> At the moment when the Ancien Régime was falling apart, when the Industrial Revolution was unfolding, artists claimed [...] the term of 'creation' as their own—a notion [...] born of the Biblical dogma of Genesis—to signify their sovereign sensibility and their free desire and to establish art as an autonomous field among human activities. (Menghini, 2021)

More recently, Materialist thought, as developed by philosophers such as Karl Marx and Walter Benjamin, opposed this tradition. According to them, it was essential to examine the mediations that enabled art (and, by extension, design) to exist in order to seize its emancipatory potential. In his essay, *The Author as Producer,* Benjamin sought to discover not only 'what is a work's position *vis-à-vis* the production relations of its time,' but, above all, 'what is its position within them?' (Benjamin, [1934] 1998, p.87). For him, it was a matter of 'pointing out the decisive difference between merely

supplying a production apparatus and changing it'
(Benjamin, [1934] 1998, p. 93). These concepts are
relevant in order to underline the limits of deep
learning technologies, whose appeal consists in
their concealing all material contingencies. To use
Benjamin's terms, these programmes can only feed
the apparatus of production without ever seeking
to transform it. In other words, they are 'reactio-
nary' and not 'revolutionary'. For example, if an
AI can 'reproduce' (create) a painting in the style
of Rembrandt—without apparent effort and without technique being an issue—it will have far more
difficulty 'producing' not only a pictorial paradigm
as strong as Rembrandt's, but also new forms of
expression that transcend the usual categories (i.e.
oil painting, electronic music, website interface,
etc.). To ask whether artificial intelligences can
create is not framing the problem correctly, firstly
because AIs are in no way magical, and secondly,
because the vocabulary of creation, when detached
from material contingencies, gives rise to an inca-
pacity to envision technique as a space of exploration, and thus, of 'production'. When consulting
an AI (GPT-3) to determine the ways in which the
illustration profession would evolve in the wake of
artificial intelligence, the designer Étienne Mineur
was given an answer that is strangely more lucid
than many a technophile discourse: 'In order to
survive in such an environment, illustrators will
have to renounce their almost superstitious reve-
rence for creativity'.[7] The issue is thus to ensure
that deep learning technologies can produce and
not merely reproduce, which echoes the intent

                   Artificial Design

of artist and designer László Moholy-Nagy in his article 'Production–Reproduction' (1922):

> Since it is primarily production (productive creation) that serves human construction, we must strive to turn the human apparatuses (instruments) used so far only for reproductive purposes into ones that can be used for productive purposes as well. This calls for profound examination of the following questions:
> 'What is this apparatus (instrument) good for?'
> 'What is the essence of its function?'
> 'Are we able, and if so, to what end, to extend the apparatus's use so that it can serve production as well?' (Moholy-Nagy, [1922], p. 289)

In light of these considerations, one can now posit that the issue for design does not consist in aiming for the total automation of creation, since scripted creation retains nothing of the Romantic idea of a divine free will beyond the immediacy of the result. On the contrary, the divergence from a mimetic (reproductive) vision requires working 'with' the artificial world of neural networks. This in turn entails redefining what one understands by the notions of creation and design. In fact, if a group of practices that challenge the assignation of techniques to principles of profitability is maintained under the name of design, the latter can then serve as a counter power to the most

7   Étienne Mineur, Facebook post, 2 August 2022:
http://bitly.ws/wNar

demeaning ambitions, providing some wiggle room and new opportunities, even in the case of techniques that, at first glance, are not conducive to exploration, such as deep learning. The different work approaches that we are proposing here all challenge the concept of the primacy or exclusivity of human creation, which only exists when situated in technical milieus, and which, subsequently, is inevitably hybridised, or rather 'equipped'. In their analysis of these issues in the field of design, researchers Lev Manovich and Emanuele Arielli consider the following questions:

> If the attribution of intelligence is a horizon line that can never be reached, one may wonder if there are human skills laying beyond that line at all: every time machines 'solve' a specific human skill, this skill ceases to be real intelligence, turning out to be more mechanical than it appeared. This may have consequences on our understanding of human intelligence itself. (Manovich & Arielli, 2021, ch. 3, p. 15)

Just as the notion of machines has (re)defined the specificities of the human body, (for instance in the history of dissection, where human corpses became anatomical material, and thus objects of knowledge) (Saint-Jevin, 2019, p. 373), computing could be seen as an 'automated mirror' of the mind, competing with some of its tasks (Chazal, 1998), and leading us to reflect, not only on the basis of its singularity, but also on what it borrows from the mechanical. This transcendence of the human

    Artificial Design

vs. machine opposition will enable us to visualise relationships with machine learning other than its instrumentalisation for productive ends.

3

CREATIVE POTENTIALITIES
Revealing the Dynamics
of Standardisation

The first focal point of opportunity that we propose to explore is the mobilisation of deep learning technologies for the purpose of revealing the dynamics of standardisation that are central to existing productions. Even though each visual generator (i.e. DALL·E, Stable Diffusion, etc.) possesses its own 'almost immediately recognisable graphic identity', they often only produce images of average quality (generated from existing data), which can even be seen as indicators of what one should not (re)produce (Ertzscheid, 2022). One must keep in mind that the worlds of design and pop culture are already imbued with the notion of imitation. Therefore, the 2020 launch of a manga 'conceived by an AI' in the style of Osamu Tezuka by a company named Kioxia is not so much an indicator of the replacement of comic book artists by these programmes than the acknowledgement of artistic and stylistic motifs that are central to Tezuka's work. Many pop culture productions attest to this tendency to repetition, such as Walt Disney feature films where animation loops replay variations on classic films with alternate characters. In the field of fashion, similarly to the example of Tezuka, the structured dataset Fashion-MNIST (2018) offers 60,000 sprites (visual training sets) from the Zalando clothing brand catalogue from which one can sort other images, or 'generate' new pieces of clothing.

While these examples are profiled for profit (or technical demonstration), one might also make use of Connectionist AIs to study the past and present, as does the programme Digital Art History, which renews Art history using computerised methods. The project *Balenciaga AI* (2018) by artist Robbie Barrat can also be viewed from this perspective. As he himself describes it:

> Using a corpus of Balenciaga runway shows, catalogues, and campaigns, a [neural] network was trained to reconstruct Balenciaga outfits from [...] silhouettes. The results are outfits which are novel but at the same time heavily inspired by Balenciaga's past few years [...]. The network lacks any contextual awareness of the non-visual functions of clothing [...] and in turn produces more strange outfits that completely disregard these functions. (Barrat, 2018)

This new fashion collection implicitly reveals, in an absurd and troubling manner, the repetitiveness of the actual fashion world, and, in some cases, the result is even more radical than the input. The distance with photorealistic aesthetics—which remains difficult to access through AIs and is deli-

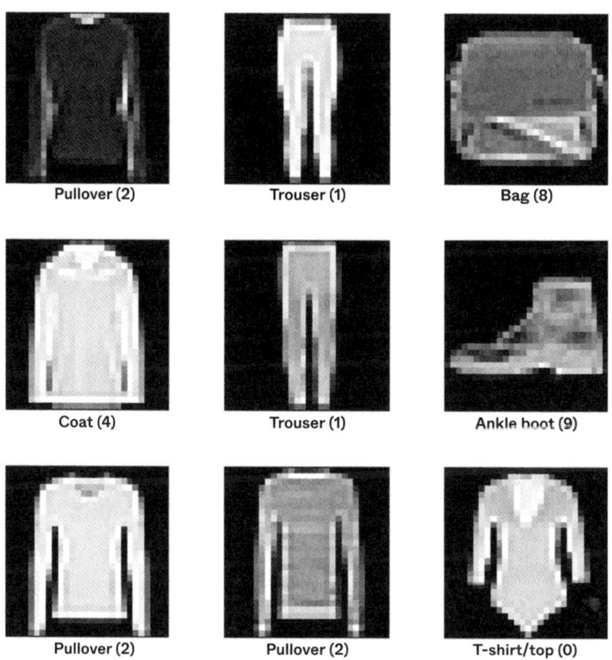

Pullover (2)
Trouser (1)
Bag (8)
Coat (4)
Trouser (1)
Ankle boot (9)
Pullover (2)
Pullover (2)
T-shirt/top (0)

berately set aside here—produces outfits that break down the customary categories of clothing: bags, suits, trousers, etc., leaving room for imagination. *Balenciaga AI* encourages us to explore what the grey areas of machine learning might be. Here, it is a matter of actualising intuitions, such as those of artist Hito Steyerl, who, in a text entitled 'In Defence of the Poor Image', urges us to positively consider images' degraded contemporary condition (i.e. pixelated, etc.), resulting from repeated editing, sampling and remix practices:

> The poor image is no longer about the real thing—the originary original. Instead, it is about its own real conditions of existence: about swarm circulation, digital dispersion, fractured and flexible temporalities. It is about defiance and appropriation just as it is about conformism and exploitation. (Steyerl, 2009)

In order to channel deep learning AIs towards the perspective of production, another viewpoint could consist in mobilising their capacity for visual analysis in order to establish unexpected genealogies between objects, as the project *X Degrees of Separation* by artist Mario Klingemann (Google Arts & Culture Lab, 2016) attempts to do. This online interface traces a fictitious genealogy between two previously selected artistic artefacts by selecting 'intermediary' works sorted by periods and which present formal

[Fig. 9] Mario Klingemann, *X Degrees of Separation*, Google Arts & Culture Lab, 2016

                Artificial Design

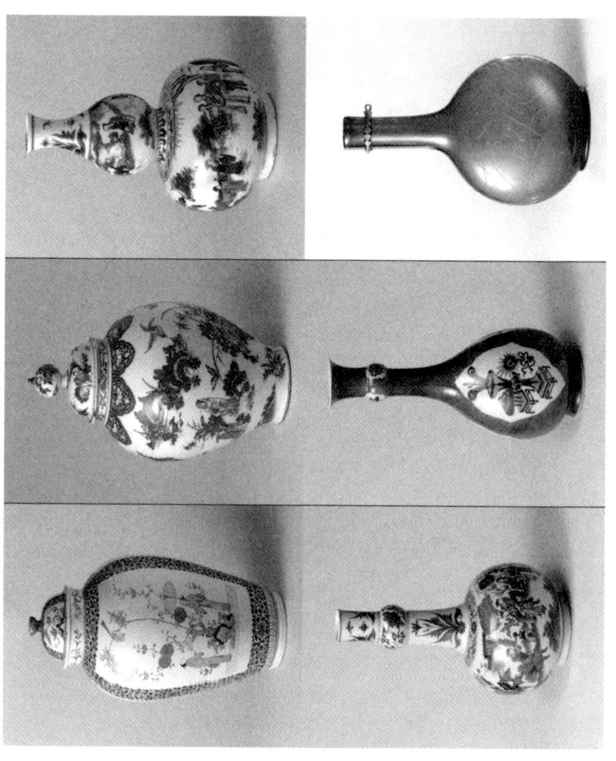

similarities (the definition of the various stages is operated by machine learning applied to online museum archives). This chain of similarities provokes unexpected juxtapositions between works of varied provenance, which, however, clash with non-Western cultures, with which these formal associations do not necessarily work. Avoiding algorithmically induced ethnocentrism is not the least of AIs major challenges (Audry, 2019).

Starting from this principle of an open, customisable serendipity, it is possible to invent systems to support decision-making for artists and designers which would enable them to compare their projects with structured datasets: similarity and dissimilarity coefficients, propositions for changes, variations, etc. Inspired by Manovich's *Cultural Analytics*, this approach would make it possible to distance oneself from requirements of absolute originality, which presuppose that artists and designers either have 'everything' or 'nothing' to say (that there is no middle ground), despite the fact that the histories of these fields show that many of the most admired works today are borrowings, copies or interpretations of works of their times or from the past (Manovich, 2020).

     Artificial Design

The second focal point of machine learning's creative potential consists in pre-empting the illusion of automation. First of all, one must resist the pretensions of digital technologies of solving more problems than they create. But beneath this apparent simplicity lies a lack of coherence and intelligibility, which is revealed during the process of creation. In a 2018 installation entitled *Of Machines Learning to See Lemon,* artists Alistair McClymont and John Fass set out coloured objects on a vast cardboard shelf with cubic storage spaces. Even though we cannot figure out its defining rules, a semblance of logic seems to emerge from this classification. Borrowing the colonial and capitalistic logic of the depiction of fruits from the artistic genre of still lifes, this work shows how difficult it is for machine learning algorithms to identify objects (when the latter are grouped, lit or oriented in different ways), and to clarify the ways in which the result (the tagging) was obtained. As the authors of the installation state, the results generated by image

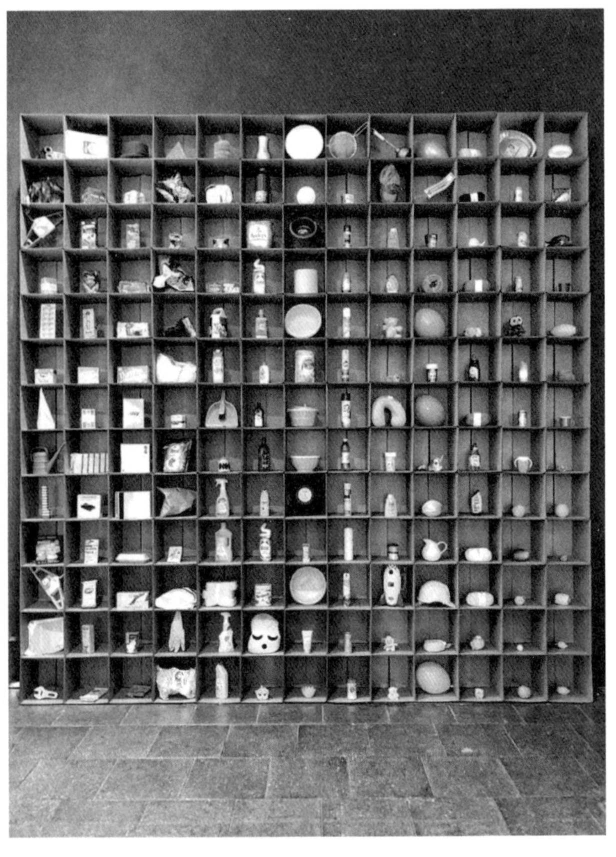

 Artificial Design

recognition systems remain 'mysterious in origin, prone to error, ambiguous in value, of erratic reliability and doubtful authenticity'. (McClymont & Fass, 2018). They go on to emphasise that:

> This invisible classification process is usually intended to produce automated decisions, which can have profound consequences for individual and collective freedom. The possible benefits of machine learning are many, but we run the risk of developing technologies of such complexity that our abilities to shape them to serve the common good are severely limited. With this installation we hope to situate machine learning as open to creative exploration and critique. (McClymont & Fass, 2018)

Two other examples demonstrate that the technical ecosystem of artificial intelligences is in no way 'immaterial'. *Anatomy of an AI System* (2018), is a large critical cartography created by researchers Kate Crawford and Vladan Joler. It visually analyses the extent of human and non-human infrastructures that enable an Amazon Echo voice-activated (text-to-speech) smart speaker to function. Thus dissected, these layers and sub-layers, which have been arranged so as to remain hidden, dispel the fantasies of a 'fluid', 'friction-less', usage, as promoted by the service industries. The promise of simplicity for the end user entails an enormous complexity that comes into play beforehand: 'Put simply: each small moment of convenience—be it answering a question, turning on a light, or playing a song—requires a vast planetary network, fuelled by the extraction of non-renewable materials, labour, and data.' (Crawford & Joler, 2018). Another example that sheds light on the material dimension of digital technologies is the exhibition *Praying for My Haters* (Centre Culturel Suisse, Paris, 2019), in which artist Lauren Huret documents the invisible contributions of social media moderators whose monitoring and selection cannot, structurally, be fully automated. Video footage shows the toxic working conditions where the obliteration of all moral sense, necessary for the execution of such tasks, replaces intelligence with a range of behaviours.

In both these cases, it is rather paradoxical to note that the simulation of human intelligence entails removing from humans that which defines them beyond biology. This resonates with the words of design pioneer William Morris, who wrote during the advent of the Industrial Revolution. According to him, it is important 'to show how far the workman is from having any share in art when he is at his work, [...] for even those who are engaged in making the wares which [...] are called 'art objects', have to work always as machines, or as the slaves of machines' (Morris, 1884). However, unlike Morris, who viewed class struggle as the only way to abolish the domination of machines over humans, modern concepts of design have shown that a range of relationships with a single technique are possible. This is the case even if economy pushes the technique in question in a dominant direction: working 'with' (rather than 'under' or 'against') machines can upend the weight of

                    Artificial Design

productivity in aesthetics, and transcend the dialectic of master and slave.

It follows that we propose to use the term 'artificial design' to refer to the camouflaging of technical operations for economic and political ends in which dominant AIs are involved. Removing this veneer would involve taking into account material conditions in the design process, along with the human labour necessary for production and its operation. Consequently, we would break with the demiurgic vision of *ex nihilo* digital creation, whose implicit connotations (the search for performance, control, and the removal of context) are ultimately rather masculine. This would be replaced by work validating vulnerabilities and attention to others. Between the lines, it would be a matter of deconstructing a certain understanding of men and masculinity as never revealing one's inner workings, one's guts or weaknesses. Emerging from this practice of concealing would mean positively embracing deficiencies, errors, ambiguities and uncertainties. In the field of machine learning, revealing underlying technical strata entails its share of difficulties, since the technical hurdles are rising ever higher and do not lend themselves to reinterpretations. According to artist and developer Nicolas Barradeau, it is important to delve into the 'substance' of machine learning, that is, the selection of various statistical models:

For artists such as Mario Klingemann and Memo Akten, it is not enough to open up programmes like Runway ML and attempt to exhaust the embedded model. What interests them is to descend into the layers in order to understand how an optimised model works, then subvert it, taking it to places where it is not supposed to go, and combining it with other systems. This 'ground-up' approach is in opposition to style transfers like DALL·E, where all you need to do is push a button. It implies understanding how the model is structured in successive layers of function calls: you can intercept a layer, invert it, re-inject another layer or some information, etc. (Mathieu, 2022)

For other people, it is not just the statistic model that should be worked with, but also datasets—which comes with its own set of difficulties, whether in terms of the necessary time or means. Media artist Deniz Kurt, in her interview for this essay, mentions the fictitious example of designing a musical website aimed at an 18-to-35 age group, where an AI trained for this type of (specifically sourced) data could potentially suggest voices or colours adapted to the given audience, or on the contrary, produce a shift in order to get rid of propositions that are too predictable (Mathieu, 2022). On the other hand, another aspect of large datasets is that their approach is holistic, and thus homogeneous. In the view of artist and designer Meredith Thomas, the constitution of a dataset opens up a new paradigm for computing, one in which programming is no longer necessary in order to obtain results: 'Instead of calling for rules, you prescribe tasks and provide data' (Mathieu, 2022). According to him, the best way to work with AIs is to create statistical models from one's own data (sketches, photos, etc.). Designer Simone Rebaudengo further clarifies this idea of personal datasets, remarking that, on the contrary, there is no need for clean and homogeneous data in order to work: 'The most interesting thing is not to obtain good results, but rather to explore alternate directions' (Mathieu, 2022).

One comes to understand that, in their drive to do too much too well, dominant AIs ultimately fail to produce specific or unexpected results. In other words, contriving to conceal the technical complexity of a system ends up restricting its actions, condemning it to the category of service. When, on the contrary, these layers are revealed, margins that allow artists and designers to manoeuvre open up. The graphic designers of Chevalvert studio (Stéphane Buellet, Arnaud Juracek and Julia Puyo) worked to that end during a workshop entitled 'Machine Jacking', where they appropriated machine learning technologies (voice recognition, text recognition, etc.), diverting them from their normal use (Stereolux, 2017). The results include the transformation of a text by processing it twenty-six times by an automated translator (Hakim Benamara), a text recognition system 'seen' through augmented reality glasses (Julien Gachadoat), or the generation of soundtracks and record sleeves based on the analysis of two Spotify playlists (Margaux Leroy). According to Chevalvert studio, putting oneself in an AI's place allows one to confront 'subjective interpretation' with the formal logic of machine learning, thus transcending the idea of substituting humans by machines. Consequently, one must deconstruct two other myths regarding so-called creative artificial intelligences: the first being that artists or designers have total control over their production, and the second that the machine can be totally autonomous. A more interesting way to proceed would be to explore the scope and location of chance when introduced into the phases of production.

Behind their promises of efficiency, deep learning technologies quickly turn out to be limited: the automation of one field does not necessarily go hand in hand with that of another, and friction between specialised programmes that are brought together underline the difficulty, even the impossibility of conceiving an abstract, global intelligence. Thus, as the members of the AI Anarchies working group encourage us to do, it is important to embrace all that 'escapes relentless computability. What still slips through? How can an anarchic AI —and an embrace of what's anarchic in AI— turn us to new possibilities for the design of future algorithmic spaces, and life alongside and within them?' (Herrmann & Vukajlović, 2022).

While the best safeguards AIs have are precisely their limits, it might be appropriate to examine how they disrupt the stability of cultural codes (Cross, 2020). When Mineur questioned GPT-3 to find out how the practice of design would evolve with AI, he found himself confronted with a proposition similar to this one: 'The way in which these programmes react to our data does not consist in following a set of rules in a linear manner, but rather in being fluid, open and organic.'[8] An astute observer of image prompts, Mineur views these programmes as 'constantly open vomit faucets' (Mathieu, 2022). However, it is their asperities that reveal these programmes at their most interesting, as when Mineur requested 'a letter 'A' in the shape of an oyster', for instance. Here, he attempts to counter the database's limitations and to look for a certain expressivity in graphic accidents, rather than in the tried-and-tested codes of science fiction and heroic fantasy. The hypothesis of a turnaround intrinsic to prediction and mechanical automation is explored in an article on the effects of algorithmic culture on creation ('Dada Data', 2018), in which design researchers Nicolas Nova and Joël Vacheron analyse productions such as musical mash-ups or covers generated by digital bots in order to show how strange, even absurd, they can be.

> It is not a question here of restoring the primacy of the author in the creative process. It is a matter rather of putting into perspective the spectre of productions and human-machine collaborations engendered by these sorts of hybridizations. The aesthetics and the coherence that spring from these productions can never be

8   Étienne Mineur, Facebook post, 2 August 2022, http://bitly.ws/wNar

fully foreseen, for they are always the fruit of a generative process that is always partially or totally random. (Nova & Vacheron, 2018)

Behind the ambition of a reliable result, the complexity of the calculations and the database's variations often yielded bizarre results: a human logic seemed to emerge, but one that was disrupted by technical operations that were impossible to clarify. The same is true of the project *Made in Machina/e* (2018) by designers Simone Rebaudengo and Sami Niemelä, which explores the permeabilities between Scandinavian design (the use of wood, ceramics, the readability of functions and construction, etc.) and the industrial abundance of warehouses in the Chinese city of Shenzhen, thus evaluating the role of designers faced with machine learning. More concretely, the components, materials and merchandise available on the e-commerce site Alibaba.com are indexed ('scraped') by a programme, transmitted to a neural network 'trained' in the principles of Scandinavian design to generate briefs, which are then interpreted and constructed by a designer (Chih Chiu) before being uploaded onto the website to be sold. This commingling, not only on an algorithmic level but also between human and machine, generates industrial hybrids: for example, a ceramic kinetic control unit that can also serve as a vase, or a lamp with a base made from smartphones. Such hybridisations directly confront the history and the fundamentals of design. What happens when a product is not created for a functional purpose but rather by a whim of

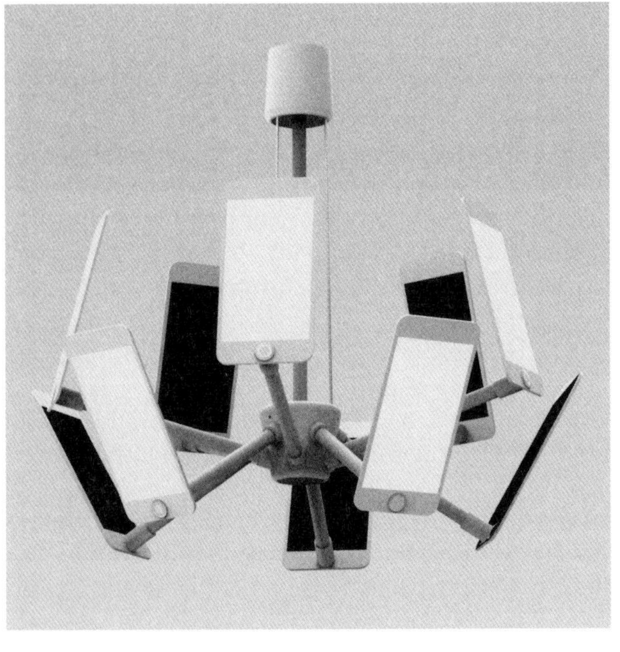

    Artificial Design

the market? Who (or what) decides what functionalities are a priority, which ones are necessary or even desirable? Does this merchandise exist solely because it is possible to produce it? (Rebaudengo & Niemelä, madeinmachina.com, 2018).

Since the predictive powers of AIs are not always exact, their results can be extremely humorous when some aspect of meaning is manifested clumsily (because it was taken too literally). The success of the Twitter account @weirddalle (*Weird DALL·E Mini Generations,* 2022) can thus be explained by the production of images that are both too exact and too bizarre when compared to the prompt (caption) visually attributed to them. Their organisation into nine squares and their themes are all part of the serial logic of memes intrinsic to internet pop culture, which involve variations on patterns shared by a given community. By questioning notions of authoriality and 'strictly human' culture, deep learning technologies reveal how formal logic produces illogic results, and how all calculations require a share of incalculable (as was the case with Turing's Machine), because it is only when the flow ceases that meaning can surface (Nova & Vacheron, 2018).

One example that does not make use of machine learning shows how the simple fact of shifting the parameters can reveal their underlying technical mechanics. As part of an exhibition (*Deus ex Machina,* curated by Sophie Fétro, 2015) at the Centre Saint-Charles, (Paris 1 Panthéon-Sorbonne University), graphic designers Kévin Donnot and Élise Gay (E+K) created a system to generate posters, where computer-aided manufacturing (CAM) software controlled a felt-tip pen attached to a plotter that filled in the surface of a font. The use of a pen that was a bit smaller than planned left flaws within the mechanical outline, creating an original visual piece. The outline of the tool opposed Baudelaire's concept of the innate servility of exact reproduction:

> When one creates a project, one doesn't use the logic of the magical reproduction of an object, what happens is a co-creation with the machine. We will seek to configure the form to be reproduced so that the machine might provide its imprint and reveal a certain form. This notion of imperfection, especially when one makes use of digital technologies, is really important. (Mathieu, 2022)

 Artificial Design

Exposing tracings and imperfections requires a sort of visual candour and even a form of translation, if one considers that the act of translation challenges the idea of an original that is set in stone (Benjamin, [1923] 1973). A fourth path of opportunity would then be to combine notions of translation (i.e. the passage from one semantic code to another) and transcoding (the transformation of a computer programme's code into another formal language). Here we touch upon the tension between languages considered as 'natural' (but that are socially constructed), and languages seen as 'artificial' or 'formal' (created for machines, but which nevertheless partially rely on human language). Deep learning functions based on cycles of ingestion and digestion of data, thus affecting its relationship with language. Before it started including images, sounds and videos, it was already part of the long history of computing literature, that is further developed in a neat approach of promising initiatives, such as Sudowrite (Amit Gupta and James Yu, 2021) or ChatGPT (OpenAI,

2022), which compose and reformulate texts on request according to a variety of indications: generating a description, changing the tone, summarising or lengthening a content, etc. However, could one take this a step further and invest computer code with a means to define and work on cultural 'codes' implying multiple modes of expression? How can one not only transfer, in the manner of the visual 'style transfers' of DAMs (digital asset management), but actually translate? This hypothesis was examined at the beginning of the 1990s by media theorist Vilém Flusser:

> If I cannot translate, I cannot compare. [...] It is very easy to translate a treatise on chemistry from English to French, but translating one of Li Tai Po's poems into French is virtually impossible, translating Mozart into architecture is a major problem. [...] Perhaps when the science of coding has made greater progress, we will be able to create code families. Perhaps we will find codes that can be translated and others that cannot be. If we create such a catalogue, we will be able to understand many things about the human situation. At the moment, this does not exist. I only know that the theory of translation is [...] a theory for a new era. It is a major sphere of commitment, since it entails not only translating from English into French; for example, it's a matter of translating Marx into Freud, or Freud into Catholicism, or Catholicism into Neo-positivism. That is the true nature of the game. (Flusser, 1973)

      Artificial Design

Several initiatives have explored AI's ability to bring together the translation of cultural and computing 'codes'. One initial example is the exhibition catalogue *Neurones, les Intelligences Simulées* (2020), for which designers Donnot and Gay conceived 'a sort of numerical alterity, another intelligence that could participate in the book, or annotate it' (Mathieu, 2022). The project's starting point is a neural network developed by Alex Graves at the University of Toronto, which was originally used for traffic prediction, and whose first practical application, at the end of the 2000s, was recognising handwritten text. The objective of this script was to anticipate the line drawn by a pencil outline based upon its preceding points. Donnot and Gay recovered the programme's source code and used a variety of parameters to play with its loopholes and generate the drawing of the book's title ('there were often times when the neural network got carried away and things started drifting') (Mathieu, 2022) Another script offered a system for the syntactical analysis of the catalogue content. It analysed every double-page spread in the book, identifying recurrent lexical fields and their connections. Donnot and Gay consider it is important to contextualise the designer's skills in terms of his or her capacity to connect with and to understand technical, historical and cultural objects, the better to be able to subvert them or associate them in a new way —'a curation of sorts'. From that perspective, designers have a bright future ahead, since the rise of templates and automation has the virtue of selecting fruitful contexts: 'Was there really any

Frédéric
Migayrou

Corrélations, les intelligences simulées

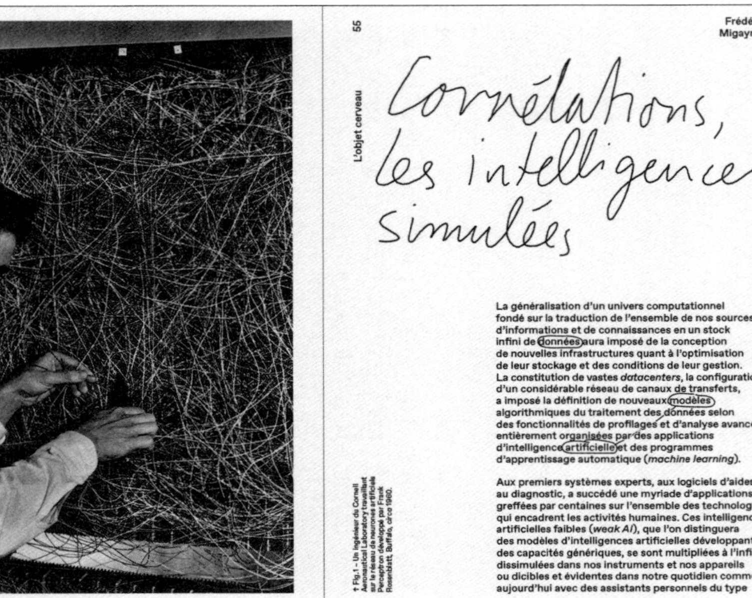

† Fig. 1 – Un ingénieur du Cornell Aeronautical Laboratory travaillant sur le réseau de neurones artificiels Perceptron développé par Frank Rosenblatt, Buffalo, circa 1960.

La généralisation d'un univers computationnel fondé sur la traduction de l'ensemble de nos sources d'informations et de connaissances en un stock infini de données aura imposé de la conception de nouvelles infrastructures quant à l'optimisation de leur stockage et des conditions de leur gestion. La constitution de vastes *datacenters*, la configuration d'un considérable réseau de canaux de transferts, a imposé la définition de nouveaux modèles algorithmiques du traitement des données selon des fonctionnalités de profilages et d'analyse avancée entièrement organisées par des applications d'intelligence artificielle et des programmes d'apprentissage automatique (*machine learning*).

Aux premiers systèmes experts, aux logiciels d'aides au diagnostic, a succédé une myriade d'applications greffées par centaines sur l'ensemble des technologies qui encadrent les activités humaines. Ces intelligences artificielles faibles (*weak AI*), que l'on distinguera des modèles d'intelligences artificielles développant des capacités génériques, se sont multipliées à l'infini, dissimulées dans nos instruments et nos appareils ou dicibles et évidentes dans notre quotidien comme aujourd'hui avec des assistants personnels du type actual creation in these areas where all one does is reproduce codes?' (Mathieu, 2022).

Rather than working with the default option of a software suite such as Adobe, tested yet exhausted by the market, it might be wiser to wonder which technique makes sense. Considered through an open approach, the spectrum of AIs is wide enough to explore the translation of cultural codes. As a result, designer Simone Rebaudengo sees machine learning as a way to explore the spectrum that exists between two given codes rather than reproducing them (Mathieu, 2022). For example, one could instruct a machine to apply a style to an object, say 40% of the style of designer Alvar Aalto, or 30% Aalto and 40% someone else, then navigate the resulting strange space in order to identify the unexpected continuities between the designers. Rebaudengo goes on to add that the technical advances of statistical models of language such as Google LaMDA (Language Model for Dialogue Applications, 2020) now makes it possible not only to converse with virtually anyone, but even with virtually anything, such as Pluto for example, who, when addressed, responds from the viewpoint of a planet. Cristóbal Valenzuela, cofounder of the Runway ML (2019) software, which uses machine learning to publish videos, enthusiastically emphasises the idea that new types of translations could appear thanks to AIs. For instance, 2D images could be transformed into 3D, or even into audio graphics. These 'hybridisations of media functions' could fuel disciplines and areas of research in the creative fields (Mathieu, 2022). This passage from one media to another has been brought to light by what could be the first poetry in French written by neural networks. The collection *Machines Upon Every Flower* by artists Gregory Chatonsky and Karmel Allison brings together two machine learning programmes to generate poems using single words, then goes on to create images from the resulting poems (Chatonsky & Allison, 2018). This work, using phases and associations, encourages us to replace AIs within a larger ecosystem that brings together humans and non-humans. Chatonsky criticises the fantasy of fully automated creation, and asks the following question:

> Autonomy underpins a logic of the absolute, of separation, whose material form consists in the instrumentalisation of everything else as a resource. But nothing is autonomous, everything depends on a fabric of other things. What is the fabric of AI?[9]

9   Gregory Chatonsky, Tweet dated 27 August 2022: https://twitter.com/chatonsky/status/1563544231540535296

       Artificial Design

This focus on the intertwining between humans and technical systems introduces a fifth focal point regarding neural networks that might be of interest to designers. The idea is to stop considering AIs as machines of creation (symbolically detached from material contingencies) but rather as one stage of production. For instance, one can use deep learning to outline or analyse the results of a brainstorming session, then compare them to existing examples, using them as a strategy for decision-making, rather than for imitation or total automation. Machine learning's speed of execution changes the working methods of design. Designer Boyd Rotgans is working on the creation of a platform that contains sixty hours-worth of videos, which can be summarised on demand into a short clip, depending upon the request (selection of a person, a colour, etc.), something that could also be applied to other media (Mathieu, 2022). Cristóbal Valenzuela in turn views AIs as having the potential to iterate (repeat a process) on a large scale.

According to him, thanks to machine learning, designers can 'feed' programmes with their productions and learn to break down their work in order to iterate their work, not just ten times, but up to 100 times a day (Mathieu, 2022). AIs can also help to bring together elements from diverse areas of expertise more rapidly, and help reduce barriers of comprehension.

On a more fundamental level, according to designer Rifke Sadleir: '[We] should free ourselves from the idea that we need to get rid of machines. Machines are not humans, but rather extensions of our own minds, since what they produce is an interpretation of what we have put into them' (Mathieu, 2022). Designer Nadia Piet sees AIs as potential 'creative partners', where creation results from an exchange with machines that allows a quick exploration of this or that aesthetic, or the generation of hundreds of prototypes on demand (Mathieu, 2022). A similar hypothesis has been put into practice by Oio Studio (of which Rebaudengo is a member): on their website, they present themselves as a collective of 'bots, humans, and machines'. More precisely, the studio officially has one non-human member, nicknamed Roby, who acts as an artistic creator. Originally, this Discord bot was used to explore new products and ideas at the agency. Now, it is considered as a fully-fledged collaborator (contrary to the narrow concepts of tools and automation). Roby has its own Instagram account, and 'lives' in a Raspberry Pi microcontroller. Contrary to the anthropomorphic approach that prevails in much of computing,

                    Artificial Design

what interests Rebaudengo in this type of process is the creation of an intelligence 'that is not as intelligent as a human' (Rebaudengo, 2016). This idea is evoked in *Domesticating Intelligence,* his series of objects which gave rise to a programme that behaved like a bird (Google Creative Lab, 2017). It is impossible to speak to it, one must interact with it through sound and gestures, by taking it outside, and so on. This opens, among other things, new perspectives on the notion of private life.

The interest for other modalities of the psyche has been passed over by AIs and by their incarnation within objects such as voice assistants. Other relationships with machines deserve to be explored, including whether one remains within a human register (Audry, 2019). Thus, Rebaudengo encourages us to ask such questions as: 'Is this a support tool? Is it a software like Photoshop? A work colleague? An intern? Or is it just a weird guy who has his own point of view?' (Mathieu, 2022). This approach was implemented by artist Raphaël Bastide in his performance Twins (2016), where he locked himself in a gallery for three days in order to develop AIs:

> [The performance became] a study on digital authorship (the relationship between the developer and his intelligent avatars) and on the emotional capacities of non-humans. Research on artificial neural networks and the progress of machine learning enables us to deepen and refine our knowledge of our own species and of the human brain. (Bastide, 2016)

If one follows this line of reasoning, AIs could perhaps become not only assistants, but collaborators, which would potentially entail profound reconfigurations of design methods (Audry, 2019). This hypothesis was explored at HEAD–Genève, as part of a workshop for Media Design Master students coordinated by Alexia Mathieu, Jürg Lehni and Douglas Edric Stanley. A collective project resulted from the workshop, entitled *Thinking Machines* (2020). Its objective was to take the opposing view of the idea of the replacement of designers by machines (Masure, 2020, p.128–131). More specifically, *Thinking Machines* took the form of a publishing system for customised narratives using perforated cards, text generators, shadow theatre, voice recognition, machine learning, and web publishing tools in order to create original stories. By mixing several periods of information technology, from its beginnings to the era of the neural networks of deep learning, 'the old becomes the new which becomes the old'.[10] This process reveals what could potentially be the shape of the design studio of the future—not so much a place where one can define solutions and fixed formats than a laboratory where one can mix a variety of techniques and make them branch out.

10 Project website: *www.distortion.mastermedia design.ch/Thinking%20Machines*

[Fig. 13] Thinking Machines, Master Media Design workshop directed by Jürg Lehni and Douglas Edric Stanley. Students: Gabriel Abergel, Leyla Baghirli, Aurélie Belle, Amsatou Diop, Laís Kunzendorff, Johan Pardo, 2020.

 Artificial Design

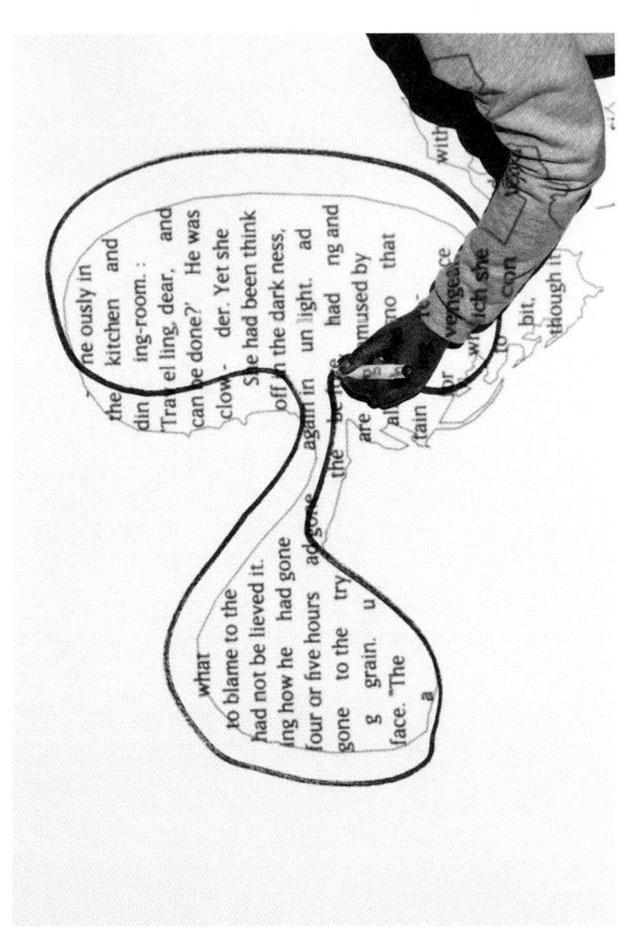

ne ously in
the kitchen and
din ing-room. :
'Tra el ling, dear, and
can be done?' He was
clow - der. Yet she
She had been think
off h the dark ness,
again in un light. ad
the had ng and
are mused by
al no that
tain
what
to blame to the
had not be lieved it.
ing how he had gone
four or five hours ad one
gone to the try
g grain. u
face. 'The
a
with
vengeance
which she
con
bit,
though

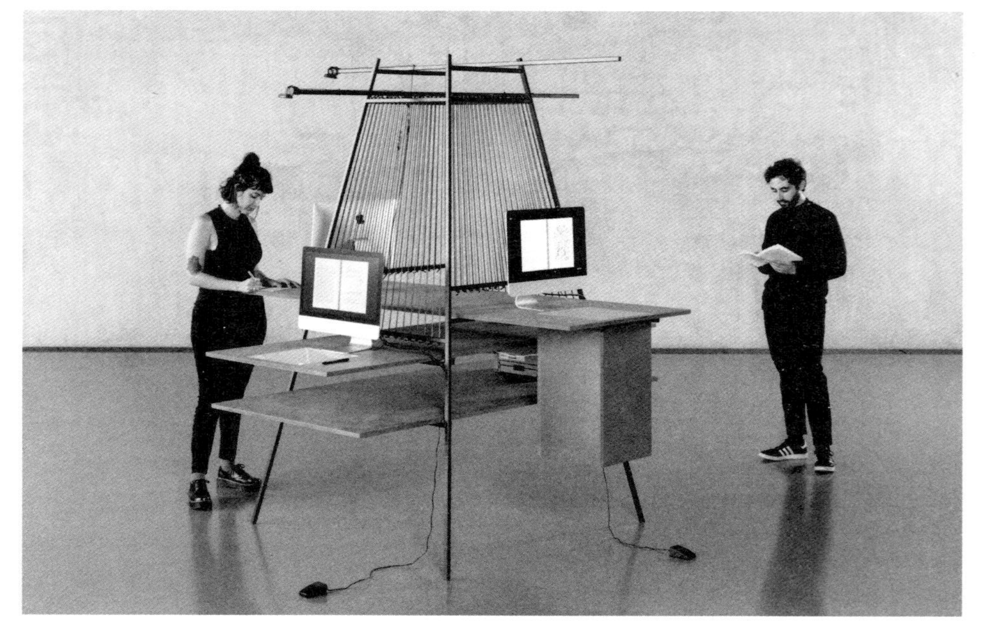

[Fig. 14] **Thinking Machines, Master Media Design workshop directed by Jürg Lehni and Douglas Edric Stanley. Students: Gabriel Abergel, Leyla Baghirli, Aurélie Belle, Amsatou Diop, Laís Kunzendorff, Johan Pardo, 2020.**

These various perspectives on the situation and the future of design faced with the advent of machine learning, lead us to clarify the meaning of the title of this essay, 'artificial design', which we understand as the desire to make the workings of a system more complex to increase its profitability. While this tendency is not confined to AIs, it has been pushed to a new level by the increased amount of layers necessary for deep learning operations. The reduction of design to a one-way street does present the serious risk of reducing production to homogeneous stereotypes, where each and every problem needs to be modelled and verbalised in detail in order to exist. These technologies tend to impose their dominant values which results in the narrowing, and even in the suppression, of future imaginations, whether dominated by a Western or a masculine vision, or by bodies and psyches that are all perfectly valid. The fantasy of the omnipotence of a machine controlled by a human goes back to older logics of domination and slavery that urgently need to be deconstructed. We must rethink our relationships with technologies, shifting from a binary (domination/execution) comprehension of machines to the apprehension of complexity and vulnerabilities. At that point, the work becomes less vertical than it is horizontal, more collaborative than it is instrumental.

For instance, it must be noted that AIs' dominant modality excludes the idea of simulating deficient (i.e. human) psyches, opting rather for the normative vision of a continually working brain (and one which does nothing else). And yet, Turing, in his prefiguration of computers, had demonstrated that all calculations inherently imply an area of the incalculable, and that all machines, no matter how efficient, will eventually break down. If one seeks to make up for, or conceal these pauses, the consequence is banning the production of new meanings and condemning these systems to mere reproduction. Deprived of its ability to suspend the flow, and thus to surprise, technique that is instrumentalised can only be a spectacle, an artifice. In French, the first historical occurrence of the term 'artifice' is related to the 'art of deception' and to an 'adroit and more or less deceptive means', to which the idea of a device prepared for a festival and intended to dazzle an audience (*feu d'artifice*, fireworks in English), was subsequently added (Rey, 2010). It is no small deception to have coined the term 'artificial intelligence' for an artifice consisting of assimilating simulated intelligences with the ability to read between the lines (*inter-legere*)[11]—something that a machine will never be able to do.

                      Artificial Design

Deep learning technologies are not inevitably doomed to be incorporated within the realm of artifice. On the contrary, it would be to their advantage to become 'intelligences of the artificial'. While the term 'artificial' might seem similar to 'artifice', 'it was only used exceptionally to signify deceptive or insidious [...]. It was merely the opposite of natural, even as it preserved the idea of a measured, methodical human activity' (Rey, 2010). Designating, in the fullest sense, what is produced by technical means, the artificial can be cultivated with a variety of approaches, as designer Ezio Manzini encourages us to do. According to him, human action and the continuous transformation of living environments have managed to demolish the distinctions between artificial and natural: the artificial has, in a sense, become 'second nature', and designers are tasked with fashioning its fate. The uniformity engendered by the media applications of deep learning is not inevitable, and they should contemplate what could become an 'ecology of the artificial'. Rather than seeking to take control ('the technical system is not an instrument [or] a means upon which a subjective will has total ascendancy for very specific ends' (Manzini, [1990] 1991), it might be more interesting to wend our way through the layers and parameters of machine learning, and to take pleasure in losing ourselves there: 'The more the technical system expands and gains in complexity, the more it will go

11   Thanks to Pierre-Damien Huyghe for having made me aware of this etymology.

down paths where it is impossible to control the end result; thus creating of a hitherto unknown artificial world which we must explore in order to assess its qualities and learn its laws' (Manzini, [1990] 1991, p.52). In short, machine learning is not just a fad to be rejected unilaterally—on the contrary, an intelligence of the artificial consists in giving up the servile and schematic simulations of the human psyche to make way for the alterity and asperity of machines.

This essay is based upon several projects carried out over the last few years, at the invitation of a variety of institutions, publications, and lectures, particularly Naoufel Abbes, Ada Ackerman, Frank Adebiaye, Anne Alombert, Jitka Aslan, Bruno Bachimont, Yaniv Benhamou, Victor Chaix, Yves Citton, Marie Doucet, Pierre-Damien Huyghe, Béatrice Joyeux-Prunel, Marie Lechner, Jürg Lehni, Alice Leroy, Claudia Mareis, Alexia Mathieu, Maël Montévil, Yann Moulier-Boutang, Vanessa Nurock, Saul Pandelakis, Vincent Puig, Emanuele Quinz, Simon Renaud, Alexandre Saint-Jevin, Antonio Somaini, Douglas Edric Stanley. I would also like to thank the following people for their invaluable advice and feedback: Frank Adebiaye, Javier Fernandez Contreras, Justine Emard, Julie Enckell Julliard, Sylvain Menétrey, Nicolas Nova, Saul Pandelakis.

Excerpts of the interviews reproduced in this essay were obtained through the research project 'Design and Machine Learning: Automation Takes Command'. HEAD–Genève team: Anthony Masure (grant applicant), Alexia Mathieu, Douglas Edric Stanley. Financing courtesy of HES·SO, Digital Transition and Societal Issues Fund, January to December 2022. The complete interviews can be found on the project website, which also features a copy of this essay with an associated chatbot: www.design-machine-learning.ch

Bibliography

Audry, Sofian, *Art in the Age of Machine Learning,* Cambridge, MIT Press, 2021

Baudelaire, Charles, 'Le public moderne et la photographie' [1859], *Études photographiques,* May 1999, journals.openedition.org/etudesphotographiques/185

Barrat, Robbie, 'Balenciaga AI', *GitHub,* 2018, robbiebarrat.github.io/balenciaga.html

Bastide, Raphaël, 'Twins', 2016, raphaelbastide.com/twins

Benhamou, Yaniv, 'Art génératif, *prompt art* et intelligence artificielle: que dit le droit d'auteur?', *Heidi News,* October 2022, heidi.news/cyber/art-generatif-prompt-art-et-intelligence-artificielle-que-dit-le-droit-d-auteur

Benjamin, Walter, 'The Task of the Translator: An Introduction to the Translation of Baudelaire's 'Tableaux Parisiens'' [1923] in *Walter Benjamin: Illuminations,* Hannah Arendt ed., Harry Zohn, trans., London, Fontana/Collins, 1973

Benjamin, Walter, 'The Author as Producer', [1934], in *Understanding Brecht,* Anna Bostock, trans., London, Verso, 1998, pp. 85–104, archive.org/details/benjamin-walter-understanding-brecht-146p/

Bratton, Benjamin H., 'The Black Stack', *E-flux,* n° 53, March 2014, e-flux.com/journal/53/59883/the-black-stack

Bush, Vannevar, 'As We May Think', *The Atlantic Monthly,* vol. 176, n° 1, July 1945

Cardon, Dominique, *À quoi rêvent les algorithmes? Nos vies à l'heure des big data,* Paris, Seuil, 2015

Cardon, Dominique, Cointet, Jean-Philippe, Mazières, Antoine, 'La revanche des neurones', *Réseaux,* n° 211, November 2018, neurovenge.antonomase.fr

Casilli, Antonio A., *En attendant les robots. Enquête sur le travail du clic,* Paris, Seuil, La Couleur des Idées collection, 2019

Cassou-Noguès, Pierre, 'Le temps et la mémoire, l'homme et la machine: autour de la cybernétique', *Intellectica,* n° 52, 2009, persee.fr/doc/intel_0769-4113_2009_num_52_2_1203

Chatonsky, Grégory, Karmel, Allison, *Machines Upon Every Flower,* Montreal, Anteism, 2018 anteism.com/shop/machines-upon-every-flower

Chazal, Gérard, *Le miroir automate: Introduction à une philosophie de l'informatique,* Paris, Champ Vallon, 1998

Christie's, 'Is Artificial Intelligence Set To Become Art's Next Medium?', *Christies.com,* December 2018, christies.com/features/A-collaboration-between-two-artists-one-human-one-a-machine-9332-1.aspx

Crawford, Kate, *Atlas of AI: Power, Politics, and the Planetary Costs of Artificial Intelligence,* Yale University Press, 2021.

Crawford, Kate, Vladan, Joler, *Anatomy of an AI System: The Amazon Echo As An Anatomical Map of Human Labor, Data and Planetary Resources,* AI Now Institute and Share Lab, 2018, anatomyof.ai

Crawford, Kate, Paglen,Trevor, *Excavating AI: The Politics of Images in Machine Learning Training Sets,* 2019, excavating.ai

Cross, Tim, 'An Understanding of AI's Limitations is Starting to Sink In', *The Economist,* 11 July 2020, economist.com/technology-quarterly/2020/06/11/an-understanding-of-ais-limitations-is-starting-to-sink-in

Ertzscheid, Olivier, 'Trump, Google, l'idiot utile, les architectures techniques toxiques et le meilleur des algorithmes possibles', *Affordance.info,* December 2018, affordance.info/mon_weblog/2018/12/meilleur-algorithmes-possibles-trump-idiot.html

Ertzscheid, Olivier, 'Une question de génération: Vers un capitalisme sémiotique', Framasoft, *Affordance,* October 2022, affordance.framasoft.org/2022/10/question-generation-capitalisme-semiotique/

Flusser, Vilém, *Le monde codifié,* Paris, Institut de l'Environnement, 1973, pp. 22-23. Unpublished offprint preserved at the Vilém Flusser Archives, Universität der Künste, Berlin

Herrmann, Clara, Vukajlović Nataša (ed.), *AI Anarchies,* Berlin, Akademie der Künste / Junge Akademie, Autumn School, October 2022, aianarchies.smapply.io/prog/ai_anarchies aianarchies.net/about

Hinton, Geoffrey E., Osindero, Simon, Teh, Yee-Whye, 'A Fast Learning Algorithm for Deep Belief Nets', *Neural Computation,* Cambridge, MIT Press, vol. 18, n° 7, July 2006, cs.toronto.edu/~hinton/absps/fastnc.pdf

Huyghe, Pierre-Damien, 'Art et mécanique', *Le Portique,* 1999, leportique.revues.org/index296.html

Huyghe Pierre-Damien,
'De la mécanisation au design',
Azimuts, n° 39, Saint-Étienne,
ESADSE, 2013,
revue-azimuts.fr/numeros/39/
de-la-mecanisation-au-design

Huyghe, Pierre-Damien,
*Numérique. La tentation du
service,* Paris, B42, 2022

ING, 'Rembrandt Goes Digital',
ING.com, April 2016,
ing.com/Newsroom/News/
Rembrandt-goes-digital-.htm

Jorion, Paul, 'Turing, ou la
tentation de comprendre',
L'Homme, n° 153,
January–March 2000,
journals.openedition.org/
lhomme/18

Kauffman Jordan, 'Dessiner
avec l'ordinateur dans les
années soixante: le design
et ses pratiques à l'aube de
l'ère numérique', *Livraisons
de l'histoire de l'architecture,*
2016, n° 32, pp. 105–123,
problemata.org/fr/articles/640

Keller, Milo, Gunti,
Claus, Amoser, Florian,
ed., *Automated Photography,*
Lausanne, ECAL, 2021

Klein, Judy L., Lemov, Rebecca,
Gordin, Michael D., Daston,
Lorraine, Erickson, Paul, Sturm
Thomas, *How Reason Almost
Lost Its Mind: The Strange
Career of Cold War Rationality,*
Chicago, University of Chicago
Press, 2013

Kurenkov, Andrey,
'A 'Brief' History of Neural
Nets and Deep Learning',
AndreyKurenkov.com,
December 2015,
andreykurenkov.com/writing/
ai/a-brief-history-of-neural-
nets-and-deep-learning

Lacan, Jacques, *Le Séminaire,
Livre II, Le moi dans la théorie
de Freud et dans la technique
de la psychanalyse (1954–1955),*
Paris, Seuil, Champ Freudien
collection, 1978

Lassègue, Jean, 'Of Lattices,
Grids, Strips and Tape: Alan
Turing's Machines', [interview
with Kévin Donnot and Anthony
Masure], Aviva Cashmira
Kakar, trans., *Back Office,*
n° 2, 'Thinking, Classifying,
Describing', Paris, B42, 2018,
revue-backoffice.com/en/
issues/02-thinking-classfying-
displaying/jean-lassegue-grilles

Le Cun, Yann, Boser, Bernhard,
Denker, John S., Henderson,
Donnie, 'Backpropagation
Applied to Handwritten Zip
Code Recognition', *Neural
Computation,* vol. 1, n° 4,
Winter 1989,
doi.org/10.1162/neco.1989.1.4.541

Lovink, Geert, 'Proposition
on Peak Data', *Net Critique,*
April 2022, Amsterdam,
Institute of Network Cultures,
networkcultures.org/geert/2022/
04/07/proposition-on-peak-data

Maeda, John, 'Time-Graphics',
'Reactive-Graphics',

'Metadesigning', series of three essays, Tokyo, Kabushiki Kaisha, *MdN,* 1995, maedastudio.com/1995/mdn3/index.php

Manovich, Lev, Arielli, Emanuele, *Artificial Aesthetics: A Critical Guide to AI, Media and Design,* open access publication, 2021 manovich.net/content/04-projects/166-artificial-aesthetics-book/artificial_aesthetics.chapter_1.pdf

Manovich, Lev, *Cultural Analytics,* Cambridge, MIT Press, 2020

Manzini, Ezio, *Vers une écologie de l'environnement artificiel [1990],* Adriana Pilia trans., Paris, Centre Georges Pompidou, CCI, 1991

Masure, Anthony, 'Résister aux boîtes noires: Design et intelligence artificielle', Paris, PUF Cités, n° 80, *L'intelligence artificielle: enjeux éthiques et politiques,* Vanessa Nurock, ed., December 2019, anthonymasure.com/articles/2019-12-resister-boites-noires-design-intelligences-artificielles

Masure, Anthony, 'Pour un design alternatif de l'IA?', interview with Douglas Edric Stanley and Jürg Lehni, *Multitudes,* n° 78, 'Cultivons nos intelligences artificielles', 2020, anthonymasure.com/articles/2020-04-design-alternatif-ia

Masure, Anthony, 'Des premières interfaces graphiques aux intelligences artificielles du deep learning: vers un design à sens unique?' in Fenoglio Antoine, Fleury Cynthia, ed., *Soigner le monde. Design et éthique du care,* Paris, PUF, 2023a

Masure, Anthony, 'Promesses, limites, bifurcations: du 'design pour la vie' aux angles morts du numérique' in *Angles morts du numérique ubiquitaire: Un glossaire critique et amoureux,* Yves Citton, Marie Lechner, Anthony Masure, ed., Paris, ArTeC, 2023b

Mathieu, Alexia, Interviews for the research project Design and Machine Learning: Automation Takes Command, HEAD–Genève (HES·SO), January–October 2022, design-machine-learning.com

McClymont, Alistair, Fass, John, 'Of Machines Learning to See Lemon', *Alistair McClymont,* 2018, alistairmcclymont.com/artwork/of-machines-learning-to-see-lemon

McCarthy, John, Minsky, Marvin L., Rochester, Nathaniel, Shannon, Claude E., 'A Proposal for the Dartmouth Summer Research Project on Artificial Intelligence' [1955], *AI Magazine,* vol. 27, n° 4, Winter 2006, doi.org/10.1609/aimag.v27i4.1904

Menghini, Mathieu, 'Création ou production?', Geneva, *Le Courrier,* 2021, lecourrier.ch/2021/08/06/ creation-ou-production

Minsky, Marvin, Papert, Seymour, *Perceptrons: An Introduction to Computational Geometry,* Boston, MIT Press, 1969

Moholy-Nagy, László, 'Production–Reproduction' [1922], in *Moholy-Nagy,* Krisztina Passuth, ed., Eva Grusz et al trans., London, Thames and Hudson, 1985, monoskop.org/images/8/82/ Moholy-Nagy_Laszlo_1922_ Production-Reproduction.pdf

Morozov, Evgeny, *To Save Everything, Click Here: The Folly of Technological Solutionsim,* New York, PublicAffairs, 2013

Morris William, 'Art or No Art? Who Shall Settle It?', in *Justice,* 15 March 1884, marxists.org/archive/morris/ works/1884/justice/06artno.htm

Moulier-Boutang, Yann, Kyrou, Ariel, 'Mama IA Mamamouchi: Le dynamitage de sept idées reçues pour en finir avec le Bourgeois numérique, ce Monsieur Jourdain de l'intelligence artificielle', *Multitudes,* n°72, October 2018, cairn.info/revue-multitudes-2018-3-page-7.htm

Nova, Nicolas, Vacheron, Joël, 'Dada Data: An Introduction to Algorithmic Culture', Kieran Aarons trans., Paris, B42, *Back Office,* n°2, 2018, revue-backoffice.com/en/issues/ 02-thinking-classifying-displaying/ nova-vacheron-dada-data

Perriault, Jacques, 'Effet diligence, effet serendip et autres défis pour les sciences de l'information', International Colloquium Les Pratiques Collectives Distribuées sur Internet, Paris, CNRS, ENST, UIUC, UCSD, 19-20 September 2000

Posture, Julien, 'If You're Worried About DALL·E Replacing Illustrators, You Don't Understand The Power of Illustration', *Aiga Eye on Design,* July 2022, eyeondesign.aiga.org/if-youre-worried-about-dall%c2%b7e-replacing-illustrators-you-dont-understand-the-power-of-illustration

Rebaudengo, Simone, 'Domesticating Intelligence', *Medium,* July 2016, medium.com/@fishandchipsing/ domesticating-intelligence-f90067bd8e64

Rey, Alain, ed., 'Artifice', in *Dictionnaire historique de la langue française,* Paris, Le Robert, 2010

Rosenblueth, Arturo, Wiener, Norbert, Bigelow, Julian,

     Artificial Design

'Comportement, but et
téléologie' [1943], in
*Sciences cognitives: Textes
fondateurs (1943–1950),*
Aline Pélissier and Alain Tête,
ed., Paris, PUF, 1995

Saint-Jevin, Alexandre,
'La 'machine électronique'
de Lacan: Alan Turing chez
les psychanalystes', *L'évolution
psychiatrique,* n° 82, 2017,
doi.org/10.1016/j.evopsy.
2016.12.001

Saint-Jevin, Alexandre,
'Sur la trace de l'humain
dans les 'objets' de design',
Non-Fiction, March 2018,
nonfiction.fr/article-9264-sur-
la-trace-de-lhumain-dans-les-
objets-de-design.htm

Saint-Jevin, Alexandre,
'De la machine universelle
de Turing à celle de Lacan, en
passant par l'appareil psychique
freudien' in *La machine psych-
analytique: Théorie de la
machine lacanienne,* Presses
Universitaires de Dijon, 2019

Saulnier, Boris, 'Compte-
rendu de l'ouvrage de John
von Neumann *L'ordinateur
et le cerveau'* [1955–1956],
March 2003,
https://bsaulnier.github.io/phd/
coms.html

Stereolux, 'Design graphique
et intelligence artificielle: vers
un design algorithmique?',
Stereolux.org, Nantes,
October 2017,
stereolux.org/blog/design-
graphique-et-intelligence-
artificielle-vers-un-design-
algorithmique

Steyerl, Hito, 'In Defense
of the Poor Image', *E-Flux,*
November 2009,
e-flux.com/journal/10/61362/
in-defense-of-the-poor-image

Turing, Alan M., 'On
Computable Numbers,
with an Application to the
*Entscheidungsproblem' [1936],
Proceedings of the London
Mathematical Society,* vol. s2-42,
issue 1, 1937, pp. 230-265

Turing Alan M., 'Lecture on
the Automatic Computing
Engine', delivered at the London
Mathematical Society, 20
February 1947, in *The Essential
Turing: Seminal Writings in
Computing, Logic, Philosophy,
Artificial Intelligence,* Brian
Jack Copeland (ed.), New York,
Oxford University Press, 2004

Turing Alan M., 'Computing
Machinery and Intelligence',
Mind, n° 49, pp. 433-460, 1950.

Von Neumann, John, *The
Computer and the Brain,* Yale
University Press, [1958], 2000

Von Neumann, John, 'General
and Logical Theory of Automata'
[1948] in *Collected Works,* vol. 5,
Oxford, Pergamon Press, 1966

Watson, John Broadus,
'Psychology as the Behaviorist
Views it', *Psychological Review,*
n° 20, 1913

Wiener, Norbert, *Cybernetics
or Control and Communication
in the Animal and the Machine,*
New York, John Wiley & Sons,
1948,
uberty.org/wp-content/
uploads/2015/07/Norbert_
Wiener_Cybernetics.pdf

Wiener, Norbert,
*The Human Use of Human
Beings: Cybernetics and
Society,* Boston, Houghton
Mifflin, 1954

Wiggers, Kyle, 'A startup is
charging $1.99 for strings
of text to feed to DALL·E 2',
TechCrunch, July 2022,
techcrunch.com/2022/07/29/a-
startup-is-charging-1-99-for-
strings-of-text-to-feed-to-dall-e-2

     Artificial Design

[Fig 1] © Collectif Obvious
[Fig 2] © ING, Microsoft,
J. Walter Thompson
[Fig 3] © Cary Gabriel Costello
[Fig 4] © Cristobal Valenzuela
[Fig 5] © Lev Manovich
[Fig 6] © Apple
[Fig 7] © Shane McGeehan
[Fig 8] © Fashion MNIST
[Fig 9] © Mario Klingemann
[Fig 10] © Alistair McClymont
[Fig 11] © Simone Rebaudengo,
Sami Niemelä
[Fig 12] © E+K (Élise Gay and
Kevin Donnot)
[Fig 13] © HEAD–Genève
(Michel Giesbrecht)
[Fig 14] © HEAD–Genève
(Michel Giesbrecht)

Anthony Masure is an Associate Professor and Dean of Research at the Geneva University of Art and Design (HEAD–Genève, HES·SO). His research is currently focused on the impact that artificial intelligence and blockchain technologies have on design. He is a co-founder of the research journals *Back Office* and *Réel-Virtuel.* He is also the author of the essay *Design et humanités* ('Design and the Digital Humanities', B42 Editions, 2017). He is a founding member of Hint3rland (2022), a creative studio for the decentralized world.
www.anthonymasure.com

HEAD–Publishing, 2023

Title:
Artificial Design: Creation
Versus Machine Learning

Original title:
Design sous artifice: la création
au risque du machine learning

Author:
Anthony Masure

Manifestes collection edited
by Julie Enckell Julliard and
Anthony Masure

Editorial coordinator:
Sylvain Menétrey

Translator: ACK

Copy editor:
Phoebe Hadjimarkos-Clarke

Graphic charter:
Dimitri Broquard

Graphic design:
Alicia Dubuis

Fonts:
ABC Whyte (Dinamo, 2019),
Lyon Text (Commercial Type,
2009)

Printed by Imprimerie Prestige
Graphique, Plan-les-Ouates

ISBN: 978-2-940510-78-8

Legal deposit: April 2023

Hes·so

**—HEAD
Genève**

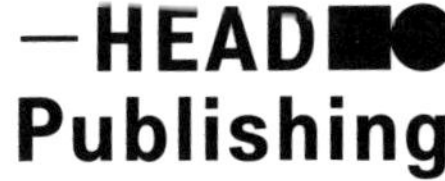

Previous publications in the Manifestes collection

Javier Fernández Contreras, *Manifesto of Interiors: Thinking in the Expanded Media,* 2021

Nicolas Nova, *Investigation/Design,* 2021

Christophe Kihm, Jill Gasparina, Anne-Lyse Renon, *Ways to Leave Earth,* 2021

Carla Demierre, *MRIOIR, MIOIRR,* 2022 (available only in French)

Anthony Masure, *Artificial Design: Creation vs. Machine Learning,* 2023

Philippe Rahm, *The Anthropocene Style,* 2023